Liszt's *Chopin*

A NEW EDITION

TO SUSAN, ROB AND JUDY

Liszt's *Chopin*

A NEW EDITION

TRANSLATED FROM THE FRENCH,
EDITED AND WITH AN INTRODUCTION BY

Meirion Hughes

MANCHESTER UNIVERSITY PRESS
Manchester and New York

distributed in the United States exclusively by Palgrave Macmillan

Copyright © Meirion Hughes 2010

The right of Meirion Hughes to be identified as the author of this work has been asserted by him in accordance with the Copyright, Designs and Patents Act 1988.

Published by Manchester University Press
Oxford Road, Manchester M13 9NR, UK
and Room 400, 175 Fifth Avenue, New York, NY 10010, USA
www.manchesteruniversitypress.co.uk

Distributed in the United States exclusively by
Palgrave Macmillan, 175 Fifth Avenue, New York,
NY 10010, USA

Distributed in Canada exclusively by
UBC Press, University of British Columbia, 2029 West Mall,
Vancouver, BC, Canada V6T 1Z2

British Library Cataloguing-in-Publication Data
A catalogue record for this book is available from the British Library

Library of Congress Cataloging-in-Publication Data applied for

ISBN 978 0 7190 8351 8 paperback
ISBN 978 0 7190 8568 0 hardback

First published 2010

The publisher has no responsibility for the persistence or accuracy of URLs for any external or third-party internet websites referred to in this book, and does not guarantee that any content on such websites is, or will remain, accurate or appropriate.

Typeset by Servis Filmsetting Ltd, Stockport, Cheshire
Printed in Great Britain
by Bell & Bain Ltd, Glasgow

CONTENTS

LIST OF FIGURES – vi

ACKNOWLEDGEMENTS – vii

PREFACE – viii

Introduction – 1

Liszt's *Chopin* – 59

NOTES – 138

SELECT BIBLIOGRAPHY – 151

INDEX – 153

LIST OF FIGURES

1. Chopin c. 1849, photograph by L. A. Bisson.
   Time & Life Pictures / Getty Images — 51
2. Église Sainte Marie-Madeleine 'La Madeleine' c. 1855, Paris (VIII arrondissement), where Chopin's sumptuous funeral service was held on 30 October 1849.
   Roger Viollet / Getty Images — 52
3. Princess Carolyne von Sayn-Wittgenstein c. 1847, daguerreotype, photographer unknown, Odessa (Ukraine). — 53
4. George Sand c. 1840. Henry Guttmann / Getty Images — 54
5. Liszt c. 1858, photograph by Franz Hanfstaengl.
   Hulton Archive / Getty Images — 55
6. The Altenburg, the house in Weimar where *Chopin* was written. Photograph: Judy Rawlings — 56
7. A facsimile of a manuscript page from Chapter 2 of *Chopin*. Liszt Ferenc Memorial Museum and Research Centre, Budapest — 57
8. Title-page of the first edition of *Chopin*. The British Library — 58

ACKNOWLEDGEMENTS

My thanks first go to the dedicatees of this book; to Susan Hall for all that we had and shared in the early years of the project, to Professor Rob Stradling, lifelong comrade and friend, and to Judy Rawlings, for her sense of fun, forbearance and unstinting support in often difficult times.

I am grateful to Marie Leenhardt of the Hallé Orchestra and Dr Jean-Claude Pascal-Ferrer of the University of Bordeaux, for suggesting numerous improvements to the draft translation. I also extend my thanks to Dr Susanna Domokos and Mária Eckhardt of the Liszt Ferenc Memorial Museum and Research Centre (Budapest) for their kind co-operation and guidance as to the evolution of Liszt's text, to the virtuoso, Leslie Howard, for invaluable insights into Liszt's music and its context, and to Professor Alan Walker for timely direction on several matters. Two old and treasured friends too deserve my gratitude: Liz Bird, for archival advice during the research phase of the project, and Ben Hoogewerf, for suggesting stylistic refinements to the introduction in draft. I am indebted to the staff at the British Library, the Bibliothèque Nationale (Paris), and the Goethe- und Schiller-Archiv (Weimar) for their patient response to queries, and to Matthew Frost and his colleagues at Manchester University Press for their unflagging enthusiasm for this book.

I also wish to pay tribute to the memory of my mother, Gladys Hughes, who introduced me to Chopin's music, and to that of my piano teacher, Jean Thomas, who guided me into the widest reaches of the nineteenth-century repertoire.

PREFACE

In its earliest manifestations, Liszt's biography was simply entitled *F. Chopin*. It first appeared in instalments of the Parisian journal *La France musicale* during 1851. A year later it was re-published in (slightly augmented) book form by Escudier in Paris, the imprint being shared with Schott in Brussels and Breitkopf und Härtel in Leipzig. A much-expanded *nouvelle edition*, in which Liszt was not involved, *was* prepared by his collaborator on the original project, the Princess Carolyne von Sayn-Wittgenstein, and was published by Breitkopf und Härtel (1879). Nearly a century after its debut, Liszt's original text re-appeared in an edition by J. G. Prod'homme (Paris: Corréa 1948).

Liszt's 1852 edition has a chequered history in English translation. It appeared first in the USA – though only in the form of selected extracts – in *Dwight's Journal of Music* (1852). A decade later, the American journalist and writer, Martha Walker Cook, provided the first 'complete' translation. Entitled *Life of Chopin* (Boston: Ditson 1863), this version went through several reprints (with revisions) before 1880. It was published in Britain by Reeves in 1877. Despite being corrupted by random, unidentified and often barely relevant reams of the translator's own additional material, the Walker Cook edition has remained the standard work, even achieving the status of being posted on the web by the Gutenberg Project in 2003. Further translations appeared: by a Briton, John Broadhouse, as *The Life of Chopin* (Reeves 1899, 1912); and by an American, Edward Waters, as *Frédéric Chopin by Franz Liszt* (The Free Press of Glencoe, Collier-Macmillan 1963).

This edition is based on Liszt's own 1852 edition. Although I have endeavoured to keep editorial intervention to a minimum by retaining paragraphing, sentence structure, and punctuation whenever possible, syntactical changes have been made throughout to improve sense and to make the book an easier read. Liszt's sometimes eccentric digressions and footnotes have been retained in the name of authenticity.

As translator my approach throughout has been a periphrastic one, putting clarity before strict adherence to what is, by general agreement,

Preface

a complex and, in places, a difficult text. At those many points where the text was at its most stylistically challenging, Edward Waters' excellent literal translation proved to be an invaluable source of guidance.

This edition is intended to appeal not only to Chopin and Liszt scholars but also to readers with an interest in nineteenth century music, politics and culture.

INTRODUCTION

COMRADES AND FRIENDS

We are now merely friends, we were once comrades.[1]

Frédéric Chopin died in Paris after a long illness on 17 October 1849 at the age of thirty-nine. Within hours a death mask had been taken, within days his heart had been removed and his corpse embalmed, dressed in concert clothes and placed in the crypt of the church of the Madeleine, the newly completed temple of *le beau monde*. The funeral on 30 October was a grand affair. The church was bedecked with monogrammed black velvet drapes and attendance was by invitation only, of which over three thousand were issued. The huge congregation, made up of members of the Polish émigré community and high society, as well as gatecrashers, was estimated at four thousand.[2] The composer Hector Berlioz reported that 'the whole of artistic and aristocratic Paris was there'[3]. Women, it was said, outnumbered the men. No expense had been spared: Chopin's pupil, patron and admirer, Jane Stirling, a Scottish heiress, paid the bill, estimated at a staggering £5,000.[4] And no effort was spared either: a dispensation was obtained from the Archbishop of Paris to allow female singers to participate in Mozart's *Requiem* performed at the deceased's request. When the service was over, a select group of mourners followed the coffin on foot to the Père Lachaise Cemetery where the interment took place according to the composer's wishes: in silence. A container of Polish soil that Chopin had taken with him into exile was emptied on to the casket, and, a few weeks later, the composer's sister, Ludwika, took his heart back home to Warsaw where it was deposited in the Church of the Holy Cross.

Chopin's funeral was intended as a public statement, lavish even by the extravagant standards of the time, of the love and devotion of the close friends and family who organised his obsequies. It was also meant to ensure that the social ambition, the artistic refinement and the cherishing of the exquisite that Chopin had cultivated in life

Introduction

remained his in the ceremonies of death. Yet, on another level, did the excess and sumptuousness of the proceedings stem from an anxiety that the demise of an artist so talented, yet so private and uncomfortable in the public gaze, might otherwise go unremarked? Chopin had, after all, lived and worked in and for a limited milieu, teaching the rich and titled and performing for exclusive salon audiences, and, during the last years, illness had curtailed contact even with this rarefied public.[5] The possibility that his career, which in Liszt's words had relied on the 'shallow and flimsy esteem' (60) of wealthy patrons, might prove injurious to his posterity was aired in an obituary notice by the British journalist James W. Davison:

> Chopin's was neither a popular talent nor a popular name . . . . . Time will show . . . whether the high reputation he enjoyed as a composer . . . was wholly or partially merited, or whether, as some insist, his genius and influence have been greatly overrated by his immediate circle of admirers.[6]

Liszt was in Germany when he read of Chopin's death in a newspaper. He is reported to have burst into tears.[7] Although the two composers had once been friends they were estranged and had not seen each other for years, a time during which Liszt had been touring as a virtuoso in order to secure his own and his children's financial future. Crucially, towards the end of his peregrinations (in 1847) he had met the twenty-eight-year-old Princess Carolyne von Sayn-Wittgenstein, an enormously wealthy Polish-Ukrainian landowner, with whom he began a liaison that was to last, in one form or another, for the rest of his life.[8] Yet Chopin had been barely laid to rest before Liszt, despite being immersed in his duties as new conductor-director to the ducal court at Weimar, embarked on a biography of his erstwhile friend. To understand why he did so, it is in the first instance, essential to examine their relationship in some detail.

Comrades

Liszt and Chopin met shortly after the latter's arrival in Paris (1831) and struck up a friendship despite their very different personalities and backgrounds. Chopin had a stable upbringing, being cosseted by his family within the ambit of the Warsaw intelligentsia and nobility; his French-born father, Mikołaj, giving him a cultural and intellectual core, while his mother, Justyna, gave him a sense of her own family's noble (if impecunious) Polish pedigree. Delicate of health, his was a

Introduction

life in which family, friends and familiar social networks were of paramount importance. In contrast, Liszt left the family home in Hungary aged nine, first to study in Vienna, and then to be marketed by his father as a *Wunderkind* across the courts and concert halls of Europe. When, after years on the road, his father died, Liszt, sick of a life as a 'performing dog' in the pay of the 'exalted' (as he put it), retired at the age of sixteen.[9] Thereafter he opted for a bohemian existence in Paris centred on alcohol and *affaires* while making a living as a celebrity piano teacher; a time when he read chaotically, and suffered periods of depression and religious mania. When Liszt and Chopin first met, the contrast could not have been greater: Liszt's private life was the stuff of scandal and gossip, Chopin's characterised by calculated restraint and carefully guarded privacy.

In terms of their professional trajectories too, Liszt and Chopin were worlds apart. The former, having returned to the concert platform (in 1832) to become one of the most feared of all the keyboard virtuosos in Parisian musical life, placed the highest value on an audience's capacity to inspire a performance, craving with a raw, almost erotic, need to connect with the public: '[The poet's] task is to move his listeners, so that his emotions find an instinctive response in them as he draws them on in his flight towards the infinite' (87).

While Chopin had arrived in France as a budding virtuoso, he came to accept that he was temperamentally and technically unsuited to the grand public occasion, his big-night nerves and small keyboard tone putting a platform career beyond his reach. Instead, he became the model professor to the highest society, and it was to members of this milieu that he dedicated much of his music.

Liszt was instinctively drawn to the radical and experimental and had a core aesthetic that was rooted in the music and artistic ideals of Beethoven whom he had met in Vienna (1823) and who remained a lifelong inspiration to him. Later, among living musicians, two made a big impact on his creative development: the violinist-composer Nicolò Paganini who inspired him to compose a new piano repertoire based on technical effects; and Hector Berlioz, whose *Symphonie Fantastique* (1830) seemed to map out a new programmatic future for orchestral music. Chopin in contrast had an already evolved musical style.[10] Having been grounded in eighteenth-century music theory and aesthetics, he absorbed the post-classical 'brilliant' style epitomised by Hummel, Italian opera and the music making of the middle-class and aristocratic salon, while rejecting virtuosity for its own sake as well as

Introduction

the use of extra-musical associations. Furthermore, from an early age (and unlike Liszt), he had become drawn towards nationalist art and Polish national music and incorporated folk elements into his music, as he wrote to a close friend: 'You know how I have longed to feel our national music, and to some extent have succeeded in feeling it'.[11] So successful was he in his use of national melodies and dance rhythms especially in large-scale works that he was hailed as Poland's national composer before he left Warsaw.[12]

Politically too, Chopin and Liszt stood at an awkward angle one to the other in a city that was a cockpit of competing ideologies and shifting categories, and in an age that proved formative in the development of mass politics. The former was a Polish nationalist, steeped from childhood in the history, literature and music of his homeland. Along with the most other Poles, he passionately resented the partitions of the Polish kingdom in the previous century that had left his homeland existing only in the language, culture and memory of its people.[13] By 1830, the political climate in Russian-occupied Poland was deteriorating and, partly as a result, Chopin, who had attracted the attention of the authorities for his nationalist contacts, left the country.[14] Three weeks after his departure the 'November Uprising' erupted and, although his first impulse was to return and join the struggle, family and friends persuaded him to remain abroad to write music for the cause. Alone in Vienna, he resolved that his piano 'would weep itself out' from exile.[15] Once in Paris, his attachment to the ideal of an independent Polish state that was traditional and oligarchic led him to associate with the exile group around the conservative figure of Prince Adam Czartoryski, the head of what was, in effect, a Polish government-in-exile.[16] He revealed his proclivities to an old school friend in a rare comment on the 'July Revolution' in France: 'I love the Carlists, I can't endure the Philippists, myself I am a revolutionist'[17] Yet he was a 'revolutionist' only in the context of ridding Poland of Russian domination. Not for him, who loathed the tumult of the mob, the radical, egalitarian, and democratic notions that were coursing through European society.

Meanwhile, having hitherto evinced no interest in politics, Liszt was radicalised by the upheavals of the 'July Revolution', during which he alternated participating in street protests with sketching a 'revolutionary' symphony. Like Chopin, although from an opposite perspective, he loathed the new 'bourgeois monarchy' of Louis-Philippe, with its brash material values and the *faux* egalitarianism of its 'citizen-king',

Introduction

and drank deeply from the cup of political, social and cultural progressivism. Having few settled views and values of his own, he reached out for several strands of thought, being particularly drawn to the Christian socialism of Henri de Saint-Simon whose ideas of political and social reform emphasised the special role of the artist in society.[18] Yet, for all his new-found social and political conciousness, Liszt evinced no interest in either nationalism in general or his own Hungarian roots in particular; he spoke no Hungarian and seemed to have few imaginative or emotional links with his childhood in Hungary.

So what was it, given their differences in temperament and outlook, that made Liszt and Chopin (in the latter's intriguing phrase) 'comrades'? Was it the fact that they moved within the same coterie of musicians, artists and intellectuals (although each had his own separate milieu) and that they gave occasional concerts together? Was it the mutual respect that the two men had for each other's musicianship, specifically Liszt's esteem for Chopin's originality as a composer and his refinement in performance, and Chopin's admiration for Liszt's technical brilliance and expressive keyboard range? Or did their comradeship reside on another, deeper level: on a shared dedication to the ideal of musical progress? Chopin declared his radical ambitions when he wrote of his 'bold but noble resolution of creating a new era in art' and 'always strive to go forward'[19] in his compositions. Liszt too, despite his restless intellectual inclinations, was committed to musical reform, to hurling a 'lance into the boundless realms of the future' (as he later expressed it), through performance, composition and writing.[20] One important index of their comradeship in art is to be found in Chopin's dedication to Liszt of his *Études* Op. 10 (1833).

A crucial aspect of Liszt's progressivism was his commitment to journalism which began with articles in *La Gazette musicale*, in one of which, 'On the Position of Artists and their Place in Society', he excoriated the state of French musical life, demanding a reform that would abolish the old order.[21] In this extraordinary essay, a manifesto in all but name, he insisted that music had a role in transforming society, a reformation in which musicians would undertake a priest-like function. Key to Liszt's ambitions was the mobilisation of a new young generation that would settle for nothing short of a cultural and social revolution. Although this essay was tinged with the fervour and naivety of youth, he elaborated upon his themes in subsequent writings, not least in his biography of Chopin, and strove to implement his core ideas for the rest of his life.

Introduction

Just as Liszt was embracing his new vocation as a journalist, his relationship with Chopin suffered a setback. Early in 1835, Liszt, who had access to Chopin's apartment in the rue de la Chaussée d'Antin, abused his friend's trust by having a sexual encounter in his friend's bed. Worse, the woman involved was the young wife of Chopin's piano supplier and close friend Camille Pleyel.[22] Chopin, feeling betrayed and compromised, could neither completely forgive nor forget the incident, and his relationship with Liszt was damaged. Under the circumstances it is perhaps just as well that, shortly after this episode, Liszt left France to elope with his married and already pregnant lover, the Comtesse Marie d'Agoult.[23]

Friends

When Liszt, together with d'Agoult (and their new daughter, Blandine), returned to Paris in October 1836 contact with Chopin was renewed, and for a time the warmth between them seemed to return. Liszt and his mistress became regular visitors to Chopin's apartment in the Chaussée d'Antin, while he accepted invitations to their fashionable salon in rue Lafitte where they introduced him to the novelist George Sand.[24] The meeting proved portentous since, although the composer's first impressions were unfavourable he and Sand eventually became lovers. Meanwhile, Chopin marked the renewed cordiality (at least) in relations with Liszt by dedicating his *Études* Op. 25 (1837) to d'Agoult. Although Liszt and his ménage were soon on the move again his correspondence reveals that he greatly valued his friendship with Chopin.[25]

It was not long, however, before the friendship was again in jeopardy, this time due to the deteriorating relationship between d'Agoult and Sand. Although the women at first got on well, Sand's passionate and (almost certainly) platonic friendship with Liszt, combined with d'Agoult's insecurities about her relationship with her partner took their toll. Although all three remained close for a time, the Countess's jealous resentment of Sand's intimacy with Liszt increasingly found expression in gossip about the writer's life and her relationship with Chopin. Matters were brought to a head in 1839 when Sand gave the novelist Honoré de Balzac insights into d'Agoult's life with Liszt, material that he used in his novel *Béatrix*. Not surprisingly, contact between the two couples ceased.[26] Although Chopin's view of these ructions is unrecorded, Liszt, later in life, blamed the deterioration in their friendship on the toxic enmity that erupted between the writer and the mother of his children.[27]

Introduction

Meanwhile, in late 1839 Liszt went to Hungary for the first time in sixteen years. Invited as acknowledgement of his charity concerts in aid of victims of the Danube flood of the previous year, he was stirred by hitherto unacknowledged patriotic feelings. He had, unbeknown to him, become the most famous living Hungarian, prized as a national celebrity with an international profile, courted by the leading lights of the nationalist opposition movement – including Lajos Batthyány, a future prime minister – that wanted far more autonomy from Austria. Liszt was overwhelmed by his welcome, as crowds, political receptions and newspaper articles, even a special biscuit (in the shape of a grand piano) honoured his presence. The climax of the visit was a concert at the Hungarian Theatre in Pest, at the end of which he was presented with a 'sabre of honour' in the name of the nation (4 January 1840). Liszt responded with an acceptance speech in which he stressed the importance of the arts in the national liberation struggle, thus unambiguously affiliating himself to the cause.[28]

Beyond the public acclaim however, there was one event that defined his return to Hungary: an evening spent in a Gypsy encampment. As he recorded, he sat on fur-skins, partook of meat, honey and Gypsy brandy, and experienced hours of music making that changed his life. It is easy to understand his admiration for the Gypsies, a people who had retained their independence despite centuries of persecution, and possessed an intuitive musicality that relied on dazzling improvisation. His conviction that music was innate, a force of nature that could not be instilled by mere musical training, was joyously affirmed that evening, as he later observed: 'Gypsy music is, for me, a kind of opium, of which I am sometimes in great need'.[29] Although he had occasionally incorporated national elements into his compositions, Liszt was so enamoured of Hungary's music that he began to collect what he believed to be national melodies for transcription and arrangement as piano pieces.[30] Although he made no clear distinction between Magyar (that is, native Hungarian) airs, Gypsy tunes and other melodies that the *Zigeuner* had made their own, he nevertheless regarded himself as a collector of 'authentic' Hungarian music and his public took him at his word. This discovery of national identity led to the publication of compilations of national melodies namely, the *Magyar Dalok* (1840–43) and *Magyar Rapszódiák* (1847), material that Liszt later incorporated into the *Hungarian Rhapsodies* (1851–53) which he conceived as an epic work of a united Hungarian people. Although Liszt's new passion for national music aligned him

Introduction

closer to Chopin's music, the personal relations between the two composers remained distant.

Given Liszt's very public conversion to political and music nationalism, it is appropriate to consider the complexities surrounding Chopin's position as a national composer. Did then his piano 'weep itself out' from exile as he had promised? In the eyes of many of his fellow-exiles his commitment to Poland was at best over-cautious, at worst half-hearted, and many criticised him bitterly for his reticence. The poet Adam Mickiewicz, for example, excoriated him for limiting his political activism to the salon,[31] while another émigré poet, Juliusz Słowacki, accused him of 'wasting his talent ... instead of sowing rebellion with his music'.[32] Other contemporaries adopted a more relaxed line; Berlioz, for example, took Chopin's 'Polishness' for granted, while the poet Heinrich Heine held that nationalism in music was too narrow a concept. Still others, like Robert Schumann, had no doubts about the political importance of Chopin's music, as he explained: 'If the mighty autocrat of the north [Tsar Nicholas I] knew what a dangerous enemy threatened him in Chopin's works, in the simple melodies of his mazurkas, he would forbid his music. Chopin's works are guns buried in flowers.'[33]

The debate surrounding his nationalist credentials has continued in recent times, with Jeffery Kallberg, Halina Goldberg and Jolanta Pękacz all entering the discussion.[34] Such scholarly disagreement both then and now is understandable since, as stated, Chopin left only tantalising references as to his political views. He rarely (if ever) sought to explain his music, wrote no programmatic works and no national opera, and had expressed no desire to lead a national school of composition. Yet surely it is a matter of degree; that Chopin's music for the cause was hedged about with caution was natural given Poland's political predicament. As a victim of a failed revolution and the 'Great Emigration' that followed, it is hardly surprising that he was not prepared to risk his family's safety and wellbeing in Russian-occupied Warsaw. Such was his mistrust of the Russians that he himself rejected the amnesties that they repeatedly extended to Polish exiles. Despite the criticism, the guns were there under the flowers, so that during his lifetime his music came to be regarded as the expression of the Polish spirit and (by extension) of the nation's will to survive. Liszt unquestionably sided with the radicals, holding that, while Chopin's nationalist credentials were indisputable, it was regrettable, even reprehensible, that his patriotism was confined to his choice of pupils,

Introduction

friendships, charity work and in the encoded subtleties of his music. It was a perceived deficiency that Liszt was carefully to address (and seek to redress) in his biography.

In the spring of 1841 Liszt, having returned to his career as a virtuoso, took a break from his touring schedule to visit his family in Paris. The visit coincided with one of Chopin's rare public appearances, a concert at the Salle Pleyel (26 April) and his first platform appearance for years. Intriguingly, Liszt persuaded the editor of the *La Revue et gazette musicale*, Maurice Schlesinger, to let him review the concert. Did he perhaps sense an opportunity to initiate a new, positive phase in his relationship with Chopin? The critic Ernest Legouvé, to whom the notice had originally been assigned, reported the switch to Chopin, seemingly with a measure of apprehension as he recalled the exchange in his memoirs:

> When I told Chopin the good news, he replied softly 'I would have preferred you'. Don't you realise, my dear friend! A review by Liszt is a stroke of good fortune for the public and for you. Don't you realise his admiration for your talent? I promise you that he will bestow upon you a fine kingdom. 'Yes', he replied with a smile, 'in his empire!'.[35]

The Salle Pleyel concert predictably turned out to be a glamorous, exclusive, and with tickets priced at twenty francs, a very expensive affair; an evening when 'all the complete aristocracy of birth, fortune, talent and beauty' came together.[36] Given the huge interest and sky-high expectations, Chopin's reputation was on the line as never before with a programme consisting of a selection of préludes and études, nocturnes and mazurkas, together with the *Second Ballade* and *Third Scherzo*. In the event, and despite the pressure, the concert proved a personal triumph – except when, after several encores, Chopin took his bows, Liszt jumped on to the stage and theatrically embraced him as if to keep him from falling. It was an extraordinary gesture which may surely be read not only as a public acknowledgement of genius, the proclamation of Chopin as Liszt's equal, but also as an act of appropriation, perhaps even of domination. Chopin's fears that Liszt was determined to bestow upon him a mere 'kingdom' in his 'empire' seemed to have been well-founded.

The concert was a great critical success, with Liszt leading the way with a eulogy that was both perceptive and well-argued. In it he acclaimed Chopin as a progressive who always 'remained himself', whose music was 'farthest removed from classical forms', whose

Introduction

genius stood 'above and beyond his fame, superior even to his success, greater still than his glory' and whose works had the 'wild and rugged flavour of his native land'. Chopin, he continued, had 'no need to shock or to show off' or engage in the 'chaotic and competitive battle for survival' that was the lot of most platform performers, since from the first note he 'established a close connection between himself and his listeners'. Yet, alongside the plaudits, Liszt suggested that Chopin's success was 'inadequate to what he truly deserves', that he did not reveal 'all that lies within him', that he was wracked by a 'secret but constant sorrow, a melancholy which hides behind a mask of gaiety'. Developing his theme of Chopin's emotional vulnerability, he went on to assert that Chopin survived the 'maelstrom' of performance only through the support of 'faithful followers' and 'warm-hearted friends' in society who protected him 'as if posterity had already made its pronouncement.' (These are judgements all that Liszt was later to explore at length in his biography.)

The events surrounding the concert doomed any hopes that Liszt might have had of reconciliation with Chopin. Mortified by the review, the Pole ignored the compliments, choosing instead to perceive malicious denigration beneath the plaudits. For him, the notice was too close to the bone, too intrusive, far too public a statement that undermined a rare moment of public triumph while confirming his worst nightmares about his erstwhile comrade's motives. The result: a cold anger that expressed itself in bitter disdain towards Liszt, as in a letter in which he dismissed the latter's music as irrelevant as the contents of old newspapers.[37]

The Salle Pleyel concert marked the final collapse of friendship. Even in better times one suspects that a level of disapproval simmered beneath the surface on both sides. That Chopin, in his heart of hearts, regarded Liszt as a 'thin-skinned Hungarian'[38] whose life was tainted by secrets and intrigues, who had an addiction to fame and honours, and who was often guilty of bad taste in pursuit of success.[39] That Liszt believed that Chopin gave nothing of himself beneath a polite and smooth surface, that he was emotionally timid, that he was an artist repelled by the frenzied face of Romanticism. Again, reservations that he explored at length in *Chopin*.

Liszt last saw Chopin in 1842. Although he tried to rescue something out of the wreckage, once writing to Chopin of his unchanged 'affection and admiration',[40] there is no evidence that he received a response. Ever persistent, Liszt even went unannounced to Chopin's apartment (May 1844) to recount a recent meeting with the latter's parents in Poland, and to extend his condolences on the subsequent death of his father. Chopin refused to see him, settling instead for a exchange of notes.[41] It was to be the last direct contact between them. Chopin thereafter disappears from Liszt's correspondence, except in a letter to Marie d'Agoult written after the publication of Sand's novel *Lucrezia Floriani* – a cruel exposé of her years with the Polish composer that marked the end of their relationship – in which Liszt makes clear how far indifference had supplanted affection: 'I thought *Lucrezia Floriani* delightful, and when I was reading it all my old affection for George returned. Tell me how things stand between her and Chopin, and if, with his malady, Chopin can go on living'.[42] The callous tone of this letter is surely indicative that by this stage the friendship between the two composers had finally died out altogether.

It is somewhat puzzling therefore as to why Liszt, barely two weeks after Chopin's funeral, wrote a letter remarkable for its cold insensitivity, to the composer's sister, Ludwika, then still in Paris sorting out her dead brother's affairs and effects, asking for her co-operation in researching his projected biography:

> My long friendship with your brother, and the sincere and deep admiration I always held for him as one of the glories of our art, obliges me to publish a few pages to honour his memory. . . . To give the work desirable accuracy, may I . . . ask you to answer some biographical questions – I would be most obliged if you would kindly put the answers in the margin. My secretary, M. Belloni, [. . . is] charged with bringing me your response with the minimum of delay.[43]

Attached to the missive was a twelve-point questionnaire on Chopin's life, asking not only for details of the early years, but also for information concerning his politics and for details of his relationship with Sand and her family. Ludwika refused, handing the document over to Jane Stirling, who unmoved by any fears she might have harboured for Chopin's posterity, replied to Liszt in a most perfunctory manner.[44] So why did Liszt proceed undeterred without the 'desirable accuracy' conferred by the co-operation of the deceased's family and close circle, and why with such haste? The answer, I believe, lies beyond any lingering feelings of friendship, but rather in his determination urgently to secure Chopin's posthumous renown and, most importantly, to define *how* he should be remembered: motives that were largely rooted in the

Introduction

tumultuous and bloody politics of the so-called 'springtime of nations', that year of revolutions 1848–49.

'MEN OF THE FUTURE'

If, as has often been proved *no-one is a prophet in his own homeland*, then is it not also the case that prophets, that is to say the men of the future who sense it and bring it closer in their works, remain unrecognised in their own times? (59)

On 6 October 1849, one of Liszt's acquaintances, the Prime Minister of Hungary, Count Lajos Batthyány, and thirteen of his generals were executed on the orders of the Commander-in-Chief of the Austrian Army in Hungary, General Baron Ludwig Haynau.[45] It was one of the final acts of the abortive Hungarian War of Independence, a conflict that shocked Europe with its savagery and loss of life. The London *Times* declared the murders 'a defect of justice, a treachery, and an excessive impolicy towards the Hungarian people'. On the same day that the report appeared Chopin died in Paris.[46]

In the immediate aftermath of Haynau's atrocity Liszt began work on *Funérailles*, one of the most political artworks of the nineteenth century – appropriately enough anticipating *l'art engagée* of the next – in which he commemorated the 'martyrs' of the Hungarian Revolution and their hopes for national freedom.[47] It has however generally been overlooked that during those same last weeks of 1849 he began work on another nationalist polemic: his biography of Chopin.

Having failed to secure the Chopin family's co-operation in preparing the memoir, Liszt was forced to do what he was very good at: improvise. Above all, he relied on his own memories along with the recollections of those who had known the late composer. One important source was the émigré and patriot, Wojciech Grzymała, a close friend of Chopin, another, as we shall see, was George Sand.[48] The Princess von Sayn-Wittgenstein, who had her own literary pretensions, was also closely involved in the project although she had never met Chopin.

The work proceeded so quickly that Liszt wrote to his German publishers, Breitkopf und Härtel, informing them that they could expect the completed manuscript in mid-February.[49] Progress, however, then stalled as Liszt began to entertain doubts about how the book was

Introduction

taking shape. Evidence for his concern is to be found in an approach a friend, the eminent critic Charles Sainte-Beuve, asking for advice and help in readying the book for publication. Sainte-Beuve, however, was not encouraging, stating that he was unable to get involved due to other commitments, and since: 'Despite its [*Chopin*] interesting appreciation of its subject, to give it form in the French language as I understand it would have required a revision and rewriting of the entire course of the work.'[50]

Undeterred by such unwelcome comment, Liszt soldiered on so that by April 1850 he was in a position to send another friend and critic, Joseph d'Ortigue, a near-final draft for comments and advice.[51] It is a measure of his determination that, despite his huge work-load that summer,[52] he pressed on towards publication, eventually opting, in the first instance, for serialisation (9 February – 17 August 1851), in *La France musicale* the house journal of the Escudier firm. As Mária Eckhardt has pointed out, Liszt then made some changes, installing corrections and changing the order of some paragraphs, before the book was published by Escudier in Paris, as well as by Schott in Brussels and Breitkopf und Härtel in Leipzig the following year.[53]

As already intimated, Liszt embarked on *Chopin* for reasons that went beyond memorialising an erstwhile friend. On a personal level, it signalled his ambition to be regarded not just as a retired virtuoso but as an intellectual, a man of letters and a polemicist, a process in which the Princess was to be closely involved. Of at least equal importance was the *way* in which Liszt wanted Chopin to be remembered. Liszt was concerned, like those who lavishly staged the composer's funeral, that Chopin should be remembered not as a 'salon' composer, or even a *Kleinmeister* of the piano, but rather as a cynosure of musical Romanticism, an outcome that might flow from a high-profile biography. Within this prescriptive project he set out to construct 'Chopin' as a bard and propagandist in the struggle for Poland's national survival while painting a flattering collective portrait of the Poles and presenting Poland's history in a positive light. Not content to promote and project Chopin as a pioneer of national music, Liszt presented him as a progressive of international stature, and by so doing posthumously appropriated him as a radical and modern for the 'New German School' in the making. *Chopin* may be seen as a biography-manifesto of national music and international progressivism rooted in the events of 1848–49, those years on which, as historians have claimed, the wheels of history turned.

Introduction

'Springtime of the nations'

On 22 February 1848, an anti-government demonstration in Paris was dispersed by troops, resulting in forty deaths. Within hours barricades had blocked the city's streets and within days King Louis-Philippe had abdicated and been permanently evicted from power. Revolutionary turmoil spread across Europe to the German states, Prussia, the Italian peninsula, and to the Austrian Habsburg dominions where workers and students took control of the streets of Vienna, forcing the Austrian chancellor, Clement von Metternich, to resign and flee into British exile. It seemed that many of the dynastic realms, so carefully restored by the Vienna Congress (1815), were on the point of disintegration.

The 'springtime of the nations' was caused by a host of factors, demographic, economic, social and political, that brought dislocating change to all classes. Nearly sixty years earlier, the French Revolution had undermined traditional, dynastic political structures to the extent that the post-Napoleonic settlement was as much about the restoration of kingship as a governing principle as it was about creating new and stable inter-state relationships. Another revolutionary upheaval in France (in 1830) heightened the sense of a continuing political crisis, while the economic depression and banking failures of the 1840s further sapped the will of ruling elites to govern. In the mix, philosophies of nationalism, the most influential being the ideas of the German thinker Johann Gottfried Herder, stressed how national identity flowed from a shared consciousness, a collective personality based on language, culture and tradition.[54] To many conservatives, nationalism presented a challenge to social stability and international peace, whereas to liberals, nationalism was a potentially liberating force, a vehicle for political change and progress. The growth of nationalism and national consciousness, and the formation and proliferation of nationalities, as Benedict Anderson has argued, often resulted in conflict, as in Spain's American empire (1810s), Turkish-occupied Greece (1820s) and Poland (1830–31).[55] The genie of nationalism was well and truly out of its bottle, and in the following decades, nationalist movements, prioritising cultural as well as political goals, and usually in alliance with liberal forces, made advances all over Europe.[56]

In Poland, nationalism, rooted in the gentry and intelligentsia, survived the partition of the state by mutating into a 'national idea, a myth, a vision'.[57] Polish hopes soared during the Napoleonic era as the Emperor's armies (in which countless Poles served) shook, at

Introduction

least for a time, the old dynastic order in eastern Europe. Although Polish hopes even survived the restoration of the partition powers, the crushing of all hope by 1830 united nationalists in support of the 'November Uprising', an insurrection that eventually brought only more repression, land confiscation, university closures and the 'Great Emigration'.[58] As a result many Poles turned to the messianic nationalism of the exiled poet Mickiewicz with his utopian belief that the 'blood sacrifice' of revolution would be finally rewarded with a divinely ordained, collective salvation.[59] Partly inspired by such heady ideas, resistance flickered in 1846 with abortive risings in Kraków, Galicia and, two years later, in Prussian-occupied Poznán. Despite the setbacks and bloodshed, Poland, with one of the oldest and most evolved national communities in Europe, proved itself to be one of the most resilient of Anderson's 'imagined communities'.

In Hungary too, nationalist ambitions had an uphill task. Although the country had been an independent kingdom with its own constitution for centuries, dynastic and historic ties had, in more recent times, sustained Austrian Habsburg domination. During the European crisis of 1848, Hungarian patriots, led by the Magyar (that is, ethnically Hungarian) gentry, challenged Austrian control. Yet Hungary was an ethnically divided society, with a spectrum of minorities preferring Austrian rule to Magyar domination. Furthermore, the nationalist movement itself was split, not only between constitutionalists and radicals but also between the Magyar gentry and those who rejected their vision of a new order based on aristocratic hegemony.[60] Hungary, like Poland, was a fractured entity and, as the revolution progressed, cracks began to show. Although the insurrection began with a moderate phase, those who demanded autonomy by any means gained the upper hand. The crisis entered its final phase when a declaration of independence (April 1849) prompted the Austrians successfully to ask for Russian military help. In the fighting that followed, thousands of Polish volunteers fought alongside the Hungarian rebels in what proved to be one of the bloodiest episodes of the 'springtime of nations'.

As stated, Liszt was converted to Hungarian political nationalism during his visit to his homeland in 1839–40. In his address accepting the 'sword of honour', he articulated his vision of how Hungary would gain self-determination and take its place among the nations: 'This sabre ... is placed at this moment in weak and pacific hands. ... Does it not seem to say, gentlemen, that Hungary, after covering herself with glory on so many fields of battle, today asks the arts, literature, and science, those friends of peace, for new illustriousness?'[61]

By emphasising the importance of music as a focus for nationalist sentiment and national endeavour, Liszt extended Herder's central notion that language was the key determinant in fixing the collective identity of a *Volk* specifically to include music.[62] It was a commitment that he, as an international celebrity, already personified.[63] During the uprising Liszt remained a staunch friend of peace, privately supporting the faction around Count Batthyány and its attempts to secure a degree of national autonomy by legislative means, and declining to make public utterances even when the revolution entered its last and bloodiest phase.

It is, however, overlooked that Liszt, like many Hungarians, also publicly and passionately supported Polish self-determination.[64] As he wrote years later, 'no one fraternises more than I do with Polish blood, the Slav ideal, Slav symbolism, Slav sentiment, Slav hopes!'[65] In his pursuit of (what might be called) a pan-nationalist cultural mission he gave his commitment to 'Slav hopes' its most remarkable substance with his biography of Chopin.

Chopin responded to the upheavals of 1848 in the same manner as Louis-Philippe and Metternich: by fleeing into British exile. Although he had other reasons to cross the Channel – the prospect of engagements to ease his finances and invitations from supporters – his main aim was to escape the barricades. As Liszt reported, 'in [Chopin's] eyes, democracy represented a collection of elements too heterogeneous, too worrying in its savage power, to win his sympathies' (101).

National poet

Liszt suggests several biographical and musical criteria to support his contention that Chopin was paradigmatically Poland's national composer.[66] As for background and personal identity, he stresses that his subject was born near Warsaw; that his matrilineal roots connected him to the Polish nobility, that Polish was his native language and that he was a lifelong Catholic. He emphasises that his first love was a Polish girl, and that, once in exile, he maintained bonds with family and friends, preferred the company of Polish émigrés and kept up with events in his homeland. Alongside (and beyond) the background detail, Liszt argues that Chopin exhibited an innate Polishness, what Trochimczyk refers to as 'psychosomatic identity', which manifested itself in a number of which different traits.[67] He reports how Chopin

Introduction

confessed that his emotional core was to be found in the term 'żal!', a tricky expression referring to a national state of mind that conveyed feelings ranging from 'intense regret' to 'an implacable malice that feeds on sterile bitterness'. (84) Although Chopin's patriotic identity did not find expression in active political engagement, Liszt insists that it was manifested in other, more subtle, forms:

> His patriotism was revealed in the direction taken by his talent, in his friendships, in his choice of favourite pupils and in the frequent and significant services that he enjoyed giving to his compatriots. We cannot recall that he took any pleasure in expressing his patriotic feelings. (100)

As for music, Liszt suggests that Chopin's connection with the Polish spirit manifested itself in several ways. Although he was born too late to have experienced the lost ways and customs of his homeland, as a child he absorbed the national spirit from elderly individuals steeped in the land, society, literature and traditions of Poland. His use of Polish genres, his fascination with national melodic and rhythmic elements, represented the renewal of the country's musical essence by an instinctive poet who had internalised Poland as a music community. In the polonaises he especially captured the 'most noble and traditional feelings of historic Poland', and poetised the 'piety', 'courtesy and gallantry' at the core of the national psyche (66). Of equal importance is Chopin's genius in communicating the mystery of "żal", that especially potent signifier of national identity, which tinges his oeuvre and 'is never far from even his sweetest reveries' (84). Liszt emphasises that Chopin maintained a musical correspondence with Poland throughout his life, and even contemplated compiling a collection of national melodies in his last years. That Chopin was a hugely important cultural and political figurehead Liszt had no doubt. As he declared:

> Many a time has a poet or artist appeared who embodies a poetic sense of people, or of an era, representing in his works that which contemporaries can only aspire to realise in their own creations. Chopin was that poet for his country and for his era since he embodied in his imagination, and represented in his poetic genius, the feelings that were then most widespread and most intrinsic to his nation. (112)

Liszt thus anointed Chopin as the singer of his nation's songs, an artist who sang with a contemporary voice, one who could stir 'as one the hearts of his people' (114).

Introduction

Of equal importance was that Liszt envisaged that Chopin's stature as a national musician would transform him into a composer of international repute, a pioneering figure who would posthumously give leadership to a young generation of national composers. He believed that such was Chopin's revolutionary legacy that he had the potential even to challenge the existing hegemony of Italian and Austro-German music and inspire a new era in musical development:

> It is likely that in music, as in the other arts, the influences of country and nation on great masters will increase with the result that the spirit of the people, more complete, more poetically true and more interesting to study, will influence its future, rather than the crude, misconceived and hesitant jottings of popular inspiration. (113)

In this extraordinary passage Liszt unambiguously set out a template for incorporating national music into canonical art music. Although national melodies had long since been collected by antiquarians, the idea that the 'spirit of the people' could, and should, initiate a new epoch of musical development was revolutionary.[68] Only the Russian composer Mikhail Glinka, in his operas *A Life for the Tsar* (1836) and *Russlan and Ludmilla* (1842) had pioneered the use of national elements in art music with a wide appeal.[69] In *Chopin* Liszt articulates the key role that national music was to have in his schema for the 'music of the future'.

Yet there are places in the biography where the reader has to doubt the consistency of Liszt's views on, and perhaps his knowledge of, his subject. In one baffling passage he seems to contradict his core message that Chopin was committed to music nationalism and the patriotic ideological movement:

> He neither studied nor strove to be a national musician, and it is possible that he was shocked to be regarded as one. Like all true national poets he sang without a fixed plan, or predetermined choice, whatever inspiration spontaneously dictated to him. (112–13)

It is hard to believe that he thought Chopin was an unintentional music nationalist. Are these remarks simply editorial oversights? It not, then Liszt's doubts add significance to his determination to construct an identity for Chopin as the national poet of Poland. Either way, in parallel with his presentation of Chopin as quintessentially Polish, he felt it essential to guide his readers to a better understanding of Poland itself, a land then little-known and rarely visited by most Europeans.

Introduction

'Land of aristocratic democracy'

In this land of aristocratic democracy, . . . how could the genius of hospitality which in Poland drew its inspiration as much from the refinements of advanced civilisation as from the touching simplicity of peasant manners, be absent from the polonaise? (69–70)

In February 1846, as part of a planned national insurrection, a revolt in Galicia led by elements of the nobility attempted to overthrow Austrian rule in the region. Before imperial troops could engage the rebels, ethnic Polish and Ukrainian serfs turned against their own gentry, crushing the uprising and leaving over a thousand of the nobility dead. Could there be any clearer demonstration of the fragility of the nationalist project in Poland, or indeed anywhere else in the Habsburg lands, than the slaughter of Slavs by their Galician countrymen in the name of the Austrian Emperor? Meanwhile, in the wider European context the butchery in Galicia split opinion: while liberals and nationalists were appalled, conservatives felt that events had demonstrated that Poland was a remote, backward, socially splintered land that deserved no place in the family of civilised nations.

European opinion had, in fact, long been divided about Poland. In the eighteenth century the philosopher Rousseau had articulated a high regard for the Polish people, writing, after the first partition, of a brave, freedom-loving and patriotic nation that would live on as a 'republic in the heart of all Poles'.[70] Herder, who first articulated the notion of *Volksgeist* ('spirit of the people'), also took a positive line, regarding the Poles as 'objects of fascination and wonder'.[71] In contrast, Voltaire held that Poland was an arena of 'farce'; and that the only chance of bringing the 'reign of Reason' to a land of such 'superstitious backwardness' lay in domination by the enlightened despotism of Russia.[72] This divergence of views continued in the next century and was particularly acute in France, where many viewed the émigrés as troublemakers at a time of political and economic uncertainty. As the magistrate Rivet observes in Balzac's *Cousin Bette* (1847): '[The Poles] want to set Europe on fire, to ruin trade and businessmen for the sake of a country which, they say, is nothing but a bog . . . . They are a kind of ferocious animal not really to be classed as belonging to the human race at all.'[73]

Rivet perceived the Pole as a dangerous semi-human, perhaps even a sub-human, other. In the same novel, the authorial voice affirms the problematic (to say the least) position of Poles in European society:

Introduction

'the Slav peoples are a link between Europe and Asia, between civilisation and barbarism. And the Pole, who belongs to the richest of the Slav nations, has in his character the childishness and instability of immature peoples.'[74] The opposition between Poland and 'Europe' rested on a persistent dynamics of polarities: 'civilised' and 'uncivilised', 'unknown' and 'known', since for many Europeans Poland was emphatically *not* Europe.

Liszt set out to challenge this negative national stereotype. He understood that Poland like his own Hungary was *terra incognita* so far as most of his readers were concerned, and assumed the role of sympathetic guide to Poland's history, society and culture. His fundamental premise is that Poland was, and remains, part of the European mainstream: a Roman Catholic nation, fascinatingly distinctive, that had for centuries defended the eastern marches of the continent against the enemies of Christendom. To support his contention he cites the occasion when Poland saved the Habsburg Empire and perhaps Europe when in 1683 a Polish army under King Jan Sobieski lifted the Turkish siege of Vienna against overwhelming odds. To understand Poland he emphasises the fact that the Poles had to defend themselves throughout their history against more powerful enemies. Poland's national suffering, both individual and collective, is a crucial subtext in *Chopin*, and Liszt's treatment of the country's history invites his readers sympathetically to examine the present. Throughout, his conviction that history had a social function and that present need should be met in accounts of the past is palpable.

Having set out the conjunctures of history, culture, and politics, Liszt proceeds to a discussion of Poland's music. Working on the premise that 'national character is revealed in national dances' (72), he explores the polonaise and the mazurka as epitomising the two most numerous classes in the national community, the aristocracy and the peasantry. In his treatment of the polonaise he foregrounds the role of the gentry nation in giving historic Poland political and social leadership, and a constitution resting on an elective monarchy, an 'aristocratic democracy', in which each noble had the right to elect his king. The polonaise he defined as both military and courtly in which the Polish aristocracy sumptuously displayed its martial poise, a dance that visually encoded the sophistication and courage that had once made Poland great. Much more than a mirror held up to gentry society, it was an expression of a national harmony that reached out beyond the barriers of class to embody the single united pulse of a whole people,

Introduction

a dance which 'in its original form . . . was no meaningless promenade [but rather] a procession in which the whole of society was splendidly displayed' (70).

Yet, as he opines, the polonaise, like the nobility it celebrated, had declined, and survived only as a shadow of its former self, a symptom of Poland's political collapse. It is hardly surprising that, as a moderate nationalist, Liszt found Poland's republicanism of the gentry compelling, since for him it combined ancient privilege with political responsibility, glamour with moral substance, tradition with modernity.[75] It is worth recalling that in Hungary the nobility had likewise powered the nationalist movement, and that it was gentry-revolutionaries who had held the nation's destiny in their hands during the crisis of 1848–49. Chopin, Liszt argues, reinvented the polonaise for the nineteenth century, placing it in the mainstream of Romantic modernity while retaining its political meaning and historical function with works in which may be heard the 'steady heavy tread of soldiers facing with brave pride all the injustices of fate' (67): a dance as repository not only of collective memory and history but also of contemporary experience.

In his exploration of the mazurka, Liszt traced the dance's peasant origins, its quintessentially democratic essence and its expression of a collective ideal. The mazurka, he argues, conveys the passion and poetry of ordinary Poles and the fragility and sometimes desperation of their lives. The mazurka, a dance in which the female takes the lead, is a celebration of the qualities of Polish women who, despite living in a male-dominated culture, are independent of spirit: 'bold, exciting and devout, loving danger, and loving love . . . they have above all a passion for fame and glory' (81). He romanticises the mazurka as a dance that empowers love and enables it to thrive however briefly in a world of pain. Poles then love more deeply, more painfully, more completely, because of their sufferings as individuals and as a nation. Here, as elsewhere in *Chopin*, the meta-narrative of suffering rooted in the injustices of history is never far beneath the surface. He celebrates the mazurka, above all, as a dance which 'reigns from the palace to the cottage' (79), an expression of national harmony and unity, declaring that Chopin transformed it into an art-form, imparting it with a new poetic depth that expressed the very soul of Poland.

Yet, for all its subtlety and passion, Liszt's construction of the polonaise and mazurka as tropes of national unity and class harmony was disingenuous. It ignored the deep and bitter divisions in Polish society, the fact that, despite its vaunted 'aristocratic democracy', Polish

Introduction

society was a site of struggle. Centuries of serfdom, landlord exploitation and localism presented acute danger to the nationalist project. In the first half of the nineteenth century conflicts existed too between modernisers and traditionalists, conservatives and liberals, monarchists and republicans and, most especially, nobility and the peasantry. The last, although the largest social class lived mostly in hunger and poverty, and with no access to political institutions it cared only fitfully about the 'national question': the bloody events in Galicia had demonstrated that. No amount of special pleading could change the fact that the polonaise and mazurka, far from bringing together the palace and the cottage, represented two different worlds.

Liszt was aware that he was writing in a dark hour of Poland's national oppression and exile, a time when myth, history and culture were vital in keeping the flame of national identity burning. He understood too that Poland as a political expression had only its history in a present made wretched by dismemberment and occupation. For a people whose future was intangible the past was known and palpable and was to be revisited, recovered and if necessary reinvented. In *Chopin* he proffers music as a unifying socio-political force, and Chopin himself as a national poet and musician-hero around whom the nation and, by extension, all nations and national sympathies could cohere. Liszt individualises Poland's pain in his subject's displacement and alienation, in his fate as a wanderer and exile, those two powerful tropes of Romanticism evoking loss, longing and occasional hope. Yet, not content with having constructed 'Chopin' as a musical property that Poles could hold in common, Liszt proceeded to craft for him an international profile that went far beyond the national.

International progressive

In May 1849, revolution broke out in the capital of Saxony, Dresden. Barricades blocked the city's streets and clashes between rebels and royal troops resulted in hundreds of dead and wounded. Once the ducal regime had captured the ringleaders and restored order, thousands of arrests followed and hundreds of revolutionaries were sentenced to long prison terms. Richard Wagner, who was active in the revolt, for one, fled the city to avoid arrest. Although the nearby Grand Duchy of Weimar braced itself for turmoil, the ducal regime need not have worried since sleepy little Weimar, the cradle of the German Enlightenment in the age of Goethe, Schiller and Herder, escaped the unrest.

Introduction

By the time these events took place, Liszt had already been living in Weimar for over a year as *Kapellmeister* to the court of the Grand Duke Carl Alexander, a life-change that stemmed from his desire to have the time and resources to grow as a composer and to pursue his wider artistic goals. He chose the city primarily because the Duke shared many of his artistic ideals and had pledged financial support for his endeavours. It also had a distinguished cultural pedigree, and could still boast of its theatre, orchestra and academy of sciences, as well as a nexus of artists and intellectuals. Ensconced in his residence at the Altenburg, Liszt embraced the challenge of re-establishing the city's reputation as the 'Athens of the North', the cultural centre of Germany. As Goethe had transformed German drama as director of the court theatre half a century earlier, so he, as music director of the court orchestra, would set a radical progressive course for German, and indeed European, music.

One suspects that, like many artists, Liszt wanted his own city, a personal power-base where he could hold court, muster his forces, and from whence he could launch his crusade. He had, after all, long despaired of the established centres of musical power. Vienna had become a backwater dominated by academic traditionalists, narrow-minded critics and waltz mongers; in Leipzig Felix Mendelssohn's legacy was being dissipated by his followers; while in Paris, the erstwhile capital of the avant-garde, traditionalist forces were regrouping around the Conservatoire, the Opéra and the decadent court of a new Napoleon. Everywhere it seemed progress was stalled as reactionary forces, commercial interests and a new, prosperous and musically uneducated public threatened to place the achievements of Romanticism in great and imminent danger. He was also determined to challenge fellow Romantics, who (in his view) prioritised classical forms and musical procedures over expressiveness and experimentation, to change their ways. As stated, Liszt likened his mission to hurling a lance into the future, a remark that recalled Alexander the Great's gesture on leading his armies on to the shores of Asia when, throwing his spear far up the beach, he declared the continent his by the spear won. That Liszt's arrival in Weimar coincided with the 'springtime of the nations' gave his mission to fashion the 'music of the future' (*Zukunftsmusik*) a dimensionally new relevance: after all, for a time the future seemed to be fashioning itself on a daily basis. Nevertheless, and ironically enough, Liszt was much relieved when the tide of violent revolution passed Weimar by,

Introduction

as he wrote comfortingly to the Grand Duke: 'Art has nowadays no need to join in the raucous cries from the barricades; its territory is purer and more exalted, and its influence at once more salutary and more lasting.'[76]

Liszt embarked on his campaign to reform and to renew musical Romanticism with a broad-based strategy based on composing, conducting, teaching and writing. At its core was his ambition to compose, and his new position gave him both the time and the orchestral resources to hone his instrumental textures and develop his own compositional ideas, especially in evolving a new large-scale form: the symphonic poem. He attached equal importance to his role as conductor, intending to revolutionise conducting with an emphasis on rehearsals and meticulous preparation, on a new expressiveness and attention to timbre, and on regarding the orchestra as an instrument in its own right. He was determined to use the Weimar orchestra to première works by other composers to help form a canon of contemporary progressive music. He also set out to make the city a centre for musical education, to transmit his ideas and ideals to a new generation of young disciples who looked to him for leadership and inspiration and who soon began to arrive at the Altenburg. Liszt was determined to advance his campaign for the 'music of the future', a phrase attributed by some scholars to the Princess von Sayn-Wittgenstein, as fiercely in print as in music. *Chopin* was intrinsic to the struggle since in it Liszt promulgated many of the values and ideals of what became known as the 'New German School'.

Liszt makes the case for Chopin's place in the pantheon of modern music as warrior-revolutionary and priest. Liszt was, in William Weber's memorable phrase, a 'musical politician par excellence,'[77] who waged his campaign for the avant-garde by drawing upon the discourses of politics and war, and whose world was peopled by friends and foes, allies and adversaries, progressives and reactionaries. Like many liberal and nationalist intellectuals, Liszt had a strong sense of a generational mission, and placed great store on youth as an agency for peaceful cultural and social transformation. He presented Chopin as a free spirit, an inspirational figure, a radical in the cause of musical liberation, 'an imperious, uncontrolled and impulsive talent ... an artist whose grace was best displayed when roaming freely'(62) He honoured Chopin's daring in inventing and appropriating miniature forms, his confidence in the piano as an expressive instrument, his

Introduction

devotion to: 'beauties of a very high order, an entirely new expressiveness, and a harmonic structure as original as it is learned [. . . and] effects that are epoch-making in the treatment of musical style' (61).

He praised Chopin for eschewing the dictates of those musical forms that were cause of so much sterility in contemporary music, while his commitment to the highest standards set the bar for future artists as Liszt declared, 'let us learn from him to reject all but the highest ambitions and concentrate our efforts on leaving a deeper mark than the fashion of the day!' (87) Liszt celebrated Chopin too as a warrior, whose inspirational resolve in the campaign for the future of Romanticism gave 'to our trials and struggles, then full of uncertainty and scepticism, the support of a calm unwavering conviction . . . a rare immutability of will as well as valuable works that the cause could appropriate' (103).

In a less combative vein Liszt also constructs 'Chopin' as a holy man of music for whom composition was a confessional experience, a place of silent communion. On this level he becomes a priest, a seer and guide, an epitome of restraint, purity, intensity and self-denial, an artist who sought nothing from the world and who had escaped from all its ties in his art: 'He poured out his soul in his compositions as others do in prayer: expressing in music those passions, those unexpressed sorrows, those unspoken regrets which pious souls pour into their communion with God' (98).

This trope restates Liszt's long-held view that a new priesthood of artists could redeem a corrupt materialistic society and restore art to a spiritual truth and beauty. Chopin is thus ordained and presented as the 'Fra Angelico' of modern music. Like the friar-painter of the *quattrocento* he is devout and ascetic, at once a progressive and conservative in an age of change, committed to exquisite workmanship and technical mastery. Had he not written all those years earlier that Romantic artists, like the painters of the Middle Ages, should be apostles of the spirit whose duty was to perfect humanity and bring humankind closer to God.[78] Thus did Liszt recruit Chopin, prophet, warrior and revolutionary, national poet and international progressive, into the ranks of the 'men of the future', who were mustering under his banner.

Chopin was arguably the most important of Liszt's literary broadsides. Although it is impossible to assess its impact, it surely helped to initiate a new interest in its subject's life and works. The 1850s and 1860s certainly witnessed a powerful new enthusiasm for Chopin and

Introduction

his music on both sides of the Atlantic. Liszt was a superb publicist, generous to a fault at promoting and projecting the achievements of other musicians alongside his own. Most, like Berlioz, were grateful for his support; a few, like Wagner, were aware of the dangers of being appropriated. Chopin too was well aware of the hazards.

For all his efforts as a cultural warrior, Liszt paid a price for his rejection of violence in the pursuit of political and social transformation. His refusal directly to become involved in the events of 1848–49 disappointed many in radical circles. Not least among them was the poet Heine who led the way in questioning the courage of Liszt's convictions; as in *Im Oktober 1849*, a meditation on the final collapse of the Hungarian revolt, where he observed:

> He will live long,
> And while Hungary bleeds to death
> The benighted Franz remains unscathed;
> His sabre also, lies in a chest of drawers.[79]

Heine's poem was intended to remind Liszt that the true artist, like the poet Lord Byron (whose memory they both revered), was also a man of action willing to consecrate his life as well as his talent to a cause. Despite such hurtful criticism, Liszt never wavered in his belief in peaceful social and political transformation. In this context, *Chopin* may be viewed as Liszt's reply to his critics as he redoubled his efforts as Hungary's most celebrated propagandist in print and in music.

The execution of Count Batthyány and his generals persuaded many that Hungary had joined Poland as a nation 'martyred' to the forces of reaction.[80] Liszt, of course, had long held that homeland's liberation struggle was synonymous with that of Poland. There is no clearer or stronger statement of his support for 'Slav hopes' than *Chopin* which, like *Funérailles*, should be regarded as an expression of longed-for statehood, and as an important politico-cultural text of the nineteenth century.

VOICES

> the public to whom a work of this kind is more especially addressed, [is] neither that of the usual newspaper readership nor that of those who reflect upon their reading, but a public between the two, consisting mainly of women . . ., plus a certain number of people who like to dream when reading.[81]

Introduction

Chopin was the first major literary project upon which Liszt and von Sayn-Wittgenstein worked. While he always acknowledged her involvement, not least by the use of the collective 'we' in the text, the exact nature and extent of their co-authorship has long been a vexed question.[82] As Alan Walker has suggested, the most reliable account of how their collaboration worked on a daily basis comes from the Princess's daughter, Marie, who spent eleven of her formative years living at the Altenburg.[83] According to her, while Liszt dictated core ideas, developing them at length, her mother worked on more general material, sketching substantial passages of her own, before her draft was read out aloud and discussed. As Marie testified, 'Liszt weighed every word my mother wanted to smuggle in [. . . and] they came to terms through mutual concessions'.[84] She also recalled that Liszt rarely conceded changes to his material. Once texts had been agreed, he made final corrections and amendments before the piece was handed to his pupils for copying (and sometimes for translation into German). Liszt then signed the finished work and, as Mária Eckhardt confirms, 'it was never a secret to Liszt's pupils and friends in Weimar that the princess did have a say in how Liszt wrote'.[85]

Things are further complicated, however, by the fact that in *Chopin* there are *three* authorial voices to be heard: not only those of Liszt and von Sayn-Wittgenstein, but also that of the novelist George Sand, with each having a subtly distinctive area of specialisation. Liszt concentrates on Chopin, man and musician – his life, character, psychopathology and the canonical and political significance of his music. The Princess meanwhile almost certainly supplies background colour and incident in passages that often contain gendered human-interest content. The third voice, George Sand, 'speaks' in those passages quoted verbatim from the novel *Lucrezia Floriani*, her fictionalised exposé of her relationship with Chopin. Liszt's own material draws upon, and resonates with, Sand's thoughts on her former lover's emotional and mental world. Apart from a few scraps of reported speech, Chopin himself remains silent throughout.

As my leading quotation makes clear, *Chopin* evolved not so much as a work of scholarship but rather as a 'little volume'[86] that would appeal to a broad musical public as an entertaining read. Surely that same public, the identical fan-base, that had flocked to his concerts all over Europe a few years earlier. Accordingly, alongside the polemics of national music and international progressivism,

Introduction

Liszt presents Chopin as a flesh and blood individual with whims and foibles, emotional needs and psychological vulnerabilities, who lived a cruelly curtailed life of joy and sorrow, triumph and disappointment.

The emperor

> 'I promise you that [Liszt] will bestow upon you a fine kingdom'. – 'Yes, [Chopin] replied with a smile, in his empire!'.[87]

Liszt is keen to explore three aspects of Chopin's private life: his relationships with women; the workings of his mental world; and the psychopathology of the consumption that eventually killed him. These strands are woven into a personal profile that provides the context in which the music and its politics are finally placed.

Liszt devotes considerable attention to the two loves of Chopin's life: Maria Wodsińska, who knew the composer in Warsaw, and George Sand, with whom he shared a life for nearly a decade. As for Wodsińska, Liszt presents her as the great missed opportunity for love in the composer's life from whom the 'tempest' of revolution tore him away 'leaving him like a confused and distracted bird on the branches of a foreign tree' (110). Liszt insists that Maria never abandoned her love for Chopin, staying close to the composer's family and remaining faithful to his memory. Liszt did not know, or perhaps he chose to ignore, that his subject had known Maria only as a child in Poland, and it was only years later (1836) that he had asked for her hand in marriage, a proposal that was vetoed by her parents. Either way, this artistic licence was surely calculated to gain the sympathy of female readers, while it also disposes of the potentially awkward question of the nature of his love-life and why Chopin never married. In any event, the lost Polish love quickly became accepted as fact, and Chopin the 'exile' from married love became an important trope in his biography.[88]

Liszt lavishes an entire chapter on his subject's relationship with George Sand whom he presents as a free spirit and a writer who transformed contemporary fiction by the realism of her work. He describes how she, a political radical and supporter of Polish independence, had set her cap at Chopin as a patriot from a nation of heroes, and resolved to nurture his genius. How, despite unpromising first impressions, they became lovers, their relationship crystallising during their winter visit to Majorca when he became dangerously ill. Liszt's narrative, closely following Sand's own account as set out in her travelogue

Introduction

Un hiver à Majorque (1842), describes how she, combining the qualities of a selfless lover and surrogate mother, 'forced back death's shadows'(124). The novelist, blinded by romantic possibilities, did not foresee the consequences of an involvement with someone as sensitive, as detached from the real world, as her new lover. It took her years to realise that underlying Chopin's charm and talent there lay a terrible emotional defeatism that rendered him incapable of returning love in a mature way. Despite her increasing disillusion, and the toll it took on their relationship, Sand continued to minister to his needs, enabling him to compose despite his declining health until she could do so no longer. When the split came Liszt stresses that for Chopin it was a mortal blow.

Expanding on passages from Sand's travelogue, Liszt draws attention to Chopin's consumptive frailty. At that time tuberculosis was a little understood condition in terms of its aetiology and treatment, rivalling cholera in its mortality rate; it was known as the 'white death' because of the characteristic anaemic pallor of sufferers. In adults, the disease was regarded as the product of an inherited disposition exacerbated by lifestyle and/or psychological factors, so that sufferers were judged at least partly responsible for their suffering.[89] By the 1820s tuberculosis had become the subject of Romantic attitudinising, underpinned by a growing corpus of literary, artistic and musical meditations on the condition. Its associations with the melancholic, mournful, decaying and doomed became powerful cultural currency, even mutating into a fashion for a while, as pale, ill, fated youth became an aspect of the 'bohemian' counterculture in Paris.[90] In this context, it is instructive to recall that, as a young man, Liszt voyeuristically visited the hospitals, condemned cells and asylums of Paris, and that this fascination with death, dying and the macabre – as well as his horror of illness – never left him.

Liszt embraces the psychological and emotional implications of Chopin's illness regarding it as a self-inflicted condition, concurring with the notion that languor of body and torpor of mind overwhelmed consumptives, once corrupted by the condition.[91] He insists that his subject gradually lost the means to think positively and write creatively and that his last years especially were characterised by depression and decline, with his music the flotsam and jetsam of a life in ruins: 'His works swirl with the passionate rancour of a man suffering from wounds more serious than he is prepared to acknowledge, just as shattered beams and spars swirl around a sinking ship' (65).

Introduction

Chopin is hereby invested with the alluring chic of the consumptive, and the imprisonment of incurable illness, the prey to a disease without hope in whose last works especially 'may be found traces of the acute sufferings that devoured him, like the claw marks of a bird of prey on a beautiful body' (65).

This programming of Chopin's music with the psychopathology of tuberculosis and depression had far-reaching consequences for how it was to be heard. The trope of Chopin the consumptive, soon entered the bloodstream of music history so that it might not be a coincidence that, within a decade, a contemporary was warning readers that the neurotic intensity of Chopin's music was hazardous: 'we have no hesitation in declaring Chopin's [influence] as dangerous. Chopin is a disease, a disease that feeds on suffering and wishes not to be cured.'[92]

Liszt's interest in Chopin's illness culminates in his morbid description of the composer's last hours. By the mid-nineteenth century, complaisance in death had certainly become one of the defining characteristics of Romanticism; the tableau of the deathbed in particular being invested with its own elaborated protocols and rituals and having an emotional power that was charged, according to Philippe Ariès, with subtle sexuality and sublimated 'erotico-macabre phantasms'.[93] In Liszt's version of events, the dying composer, psychologically and physically ravaged, is a victim too of a broken heart, which left him with 'no love as strong as death' (131).

Within this context it is instructive to recall that probably the most famous consumptive death of the age was that of Marguerite, the heroine of Alexandre Dumas's (fils) novella *La Dame aux camélias* (1848). This work, based on the real life (and death) of the courtesan Marie Duplessis, and her *affaire* with Dumas, caused a sensation in France and acquired such cult status that it was adapted first as a stage play and then as an opera libretto for Verdi: as *La Traviata* (1853). In the story, the young and beautiful Marguerite (Violetta in the opera), finding true love at last, atones for her sins before being consumed by her illness. Intriguingly, Liszt was very close to the legend of 'Marguerite' since he and Mlle. Duplessis had been lovers in the winter of 1845–46. After her death, he admitted that he was 'strangely attached' to Marie and that she was 'the first woman I have been enamoured of who is now in some cemetery or other, delivered up to sepulchral worms!'[94] Keeping close to the spirit of Dumas's novella, Liszt's deathbed tableau describes in morbid detail the farewells, the last music and the

Introduction

last rites, finally dramatising the end with what Ariès calls 'macabre affectivity':

> After a short doze, with his brow running with cold sweat, he asked, in a barely audible voice: 'Who is near me?' He then lowered his head to kiss M. Gutmann's hand, which still supported him and, while giving this last proof of friendship and gratitude, he gave up his soul. Chopin died as he lived – in loving! (135).

Chopin died, like *la dame aux camélias*, with love on his lips. At one point Liszt congratulates himself on his handiwork, opining that 'the spectacle of lingering and beautiful death has an imposing majesty that touches and attracts, softening and elevating even a soul unprepared for such holy contemplation (133). His 'Death of Chopin' must surely rank as one of the most impressive examples of its genre.

Not content with voicing Chopin's life and character, Liszt set out to 'voice' some of his music too. In so doing he chose to ignore the fact that Chopin rejected a text-driven aesthetic. Shunning the extra-musical, he declined to write exegeses for his works and resented publishers for foisting descriptive titles on his music. Liszt's gave his urge to 'poetise' Chopin's music its freest rein in his treatment of the *Grande Polonaise in F Sharp Minor* Op. 44 (1841). The main gambit of his 'programme' is inspired by Byron's 'A Dream' (1816), a poem that explores the dream world not simply as a place of disconnected impressions but as a site of psychological truth, where 'a portion of ourselves as of our time' is manifested.[95] The imagined emotional landscape is that of Byron as a poet of the extreme, the creator of lurid scenes and violent confrontations. Liszt extends his 'programme' with a description of the dreamer's encounter with a battle-scene: 'the principal theme is a sinister melody suggestive of the hour that precedes a hurricane as frustrated exclamations are heard mingling with defiance of the elements' (75). The clamour of slaughter is then interrupted by a pastoral scene (a mazurka) from which the listener is returned to the horror of the battlefield, the piece ending 'like a dream . . . with a dismal shudder' (75). Although Liszt concedes that the *Grande Polonaise* is a great work, for him the music is tainted by the neurotic gloom and pain at its heart. The implication is clear: only the music of a well and vigorous Chopin was fit for the pantheon, the wasted composer of the last years had only so much to offer the 'music of the future'. Clearly, Liszt had no compunction in exercising his imperial dominion over the deceased's now defenceless 'kingdom'. It seems that Chopin had

Introduction

managed to escape the clutches of Tsarist tyranny in life only posthumously to find himself in thrall to 'le général Liszt', Napoleon of the piano and penman of Weimar.

The princess

> When two beings become completely merged, can it ever be said where the work of one begins or of the other ends?[96]

Thus did von Sayn-Wittgenstein describe her co-authorship of *Chopin*. Although the nature and extent of her involvement can never be known, the subject demands attention however conjectural. The Princess, who was born and raised in Podolia (today's western Ukraine) and who 'always considered herself a Polish patriot and an expert on Polish matters,'[97] is most distinctively heard in the material that explores Poland, Poles and Polishness. Her pedantic style, to which her private correspondence bears ample witness, sits somewhat uneasily in the text and bears little resemblance to that of Liszt in his correspondence. As Marie von Sayn-Wittgenstein recorded, her mother was a zealous collaborator and it is not difficult to imagine that there was considerable wrangling in the Blue Room at the Altenburg before *Chopin* went to press.[98]

As stated, the national dances of Poland are intrinsic to the polemics of *Chopin,* and within this context the Princess's 'voice' surely adds detail, incident and colour with a patriotic twist. In the treatment of the polonaise, for example, there is an attempt to bring the occasion alive, to dramatise it for the reader, to convey the thrill of the ball, that ubiquitous element of the romantic novel, by inviting the reader on to the ballroom floor and into the dance. Such passages, with their attempts at colour and contrast, have a strangely filmic quality and add texture to the narrative. The same technique is deployed in describing how the mazurka is danced. Far removed from the triviality of parlour repertories and ballroom medleys, the real thing is a suggestive ritual: in comparison to the waltz and gallop, and shallow 'little love-dramas' (77) of the fandango, minuet and tarantella, the mazurka exhales the purity and vitality of pure love.

Von Sayn-Wittgenstein was ideally placed to provide much of the material on the Polish national character and the mentality of the people. Poland's women come in for particular attention; complimented for their 'diverse originality', 'wonderful vivacity' and ability to 'probe others' souls'(80–1). In order to understand Chopin's music,

Introduction

it is essential to appreciate his female compatriots, only then will the Romantic essence of his music be fully experienced. We can also, with great confidence, ascribe to her (or her influence) the many footnotes that expand, sometimes at excruciating length, on Polish topics. While such contributions were intended to reach out to Liszt's target readership, the overall effect diminishes its focus on Chopin as well as the biography's momentum and polemical authority.

It would be easy for today's reader to dismiss the descriptive and digressive passages in *Chopin* as fiction for readers of another age. The authors certainly took risks in incorporating populist elements and it is beyond doubt that the book's stylistic unevenness has undermined the work with critics both then and since. As stated, Liszt had been warned since one of his friends, the critic Charles Sainte-Beuve, alerted him to the text's flaws long before it appeared in print.[99] Yet if Liszt allowed his heart to rule his literary judgement by configuring the material so that von Sayn-Wittgenstein could be involved, who can blame him? What better way to acknowledge her as the central presence in his life than to involve her – she who had dispossessed herself of home and country to live with him in Weimar, and who harboured her own literary ambitions – in his writing? There can be little doubt Liszt allowed the Princess to 'smuggle' a good deal into his text. It is instructive to recall that when, in the 1870s, Breitkopf und Härtel approached Liszt for a second edition, after inviting the Princess to become involved (they had parted years earlier), he soon tired of the ensuing wrangles and left the project entirely in her hands.[100]

The novelist

> A microscope was needed to read his soul where so little of the light of the living ever penetrated. (109) [101]

That Liszt should turn to George Sand as a 'microscope' into Chopin's inner world is unsurprising.[102] She had lived with him for years and, outside the composer's immediate family, surely no one knew him better. Conveniently for Liszt, she had also fictionalised their relationship in *Lucrezia Floriani*. Liszt and Sand were personally close, they were in agreement on a range of political and cultural issues, and he was a great admirer of her work (as she was of his).[103] Liszt especially esteemed Sand's fiction for the daring of its subject matter and its courage in tackling complex emotions. Her work seemed to blend the emotional honesty of Balzac, with the radicalism and

Introduction

humanity of her literary hero Victor Hugo and an intuitive sense of what would appeal to a wide readership. Sand aimed for candour in her fiction and rarely in her oeuvre did she pursue it with such zeal as in *Lucrezia Floriani*.

Chopin's liaison with Sand was an unlikely pairing. Although she adored his music, she disdained members of his Polish monarchist circle, while he had serious reservations about the themes of her books (class injustice, sexual politics), and disapproved of her socialist and proletarian friends. Over time their relationship cooled: his deteriorating health became an issue between them, as did his possessiveness. Although they continued to live together discreetly, Sand began taking lovers, infidelities that caused Chopin jealous torment. When he became embroiled in Sand's quarrel with her daughter Solange (taking the younger woman's side) matters came to a head; and Sand decided to end their relationship with a novel into which she poured her frustrations and disappointments. And as if to make sure that he got the message, on one bizarre evening at Nohant, prior to publication, she read out extracts to him and the painter Delacroix.[104] The novel had its intended consequences and Chopin's bitterness went deep. As he (later) opined to Gryzmała, 'I am near to cursing Lucrezia! But she suffers too, and suffers more, because she grows daily older in wickedness'.[105]

Lucrezia Floriani shocked literary Paris. Sand's celebrity together with her unconventional lifestyle guaranteed huge interest in her work, and such a thinly disguised confessional was bound to fly off the booksellers' shelves. The novel was widely reviewed and many *literati* (including Heine) thought that Sand's vindictiveness had gone too far.[106] Such was the furore that Sand tried to distance herself from the novel's plot, insisting that her creation was entirely fictional and accusing the composer's friends of trying to turn him against her. Although Chopin outwardly ignored the rumpus, even commending the book to his family, inwardly he was 'mortified'.[107] As for Liszt, aware of the controversy in Paris, he obtained a copy while on tour in Russia and reported back to von Sayn-Wittgenstein:

> I have read *Lucrezia Floriani*, which is worth reading, even by the people who only make a light meal of products of this kind. The ideas and style are of a rare concision and clarity. The main character is in some way the authoress's portrait in prose and dressing-gown. . . . The second character, Prince Karol is drawn with subtlety and mournful spite.[108]

Introduction

In the novel Sand is the eponymous heroine, an intelligent and generous free spirit, a retired actress and single mother of four children (by different fathers) whose experience of life has not soured her optimism and capacity for love. She is a woman of the people who has made her own way in the world by dint of her distinguished stage career. Chopin is Prince Karol de Roswald, a young and emotionally immature aristocrat whose feelings for Lucrezia degenerate into a destructive possessiveness that consigns her to death by emotional asphyxiation. The biographical analogies are both many and varied, and detailed and generalised: Karol's Polish name, his cold reserve, propensity to illness, obsessive jealousy, their age difference and much else.

Given Liszt's mixed feelings about the novel, why then did he choose to draw upon 'Karol-Chopin' and present passages from the novel as biographical truth? Having already used extracts to establish Sand's pivotal role in the composer's life, he disingenuously informed his readers that, to give them the most lifelike portrait of Chopin, he would turn to some 'charming lines' from *Lucrezia Floriani* (108). It is probable too that he wanted the distinction of her reputation as well as the novel's notoriety on his side and, as stated, he was in a hurry, his political and cultural imperatives were very urgent, and *Lucrezia Floriani* was a ready source to plunder for supporting material.

Liszt's extracts from Sand's novel focus almost exclusively on Chopin's character and psychological makeup, laying bare his psyche with the force of novelistic realism, presenting, for example, 'Karol-Chopin' as an androgynous figure with 'neither age nor sex . . . a beautiful angel with the face of a sorrowing woman' (108).[109] In the same vein, the fictional character is described as otherworldly, a precious and self-obsessed figure who, although attractive to women, could not cope with love – since love for him was an act of the imagination not of the heart. 'Liszt-Sand', in short, presents 'Karol-Chopin' as a narcissistic and conflicted personality, crippled in life and stunted in love.

Liszt's borrowings from *Lucrezia Floriani* make a fine fit with his own material, and the biography benefits from Sand's direct, populist and literary contributions. In a sense, *Chopin*, like *Lucrezia*, is a fictionalised memoir of sorts, an experimental work which, although primarily intended as a work of musical history and political propaganda, was written to appeal to a wide readership. Its impact was perhaps summed-up by the leading British music critic Joseph Bennett who observed, at the end of the century: 'the Chopin best known in our time

Introduction

is without question, that of Liszt, which the Prince Karol of George Sand resembles sufficiently to serve for a confirmation'.[110]

CONTEXTS

> Chopin was slowly devoured by his own flames; his life, lived out of public gaze, being a thing intangible, revealed only in his music. He ended his days in a foreign land that he never made his adoptive country, remaining faithful to an eternal widowhood of his own. He was a poet of the stricken heart, full of secrets, silences and sorrows. (136)

We live in an age fascinated by the lives of others. Book publishing, reality television, the red-top press, the paparazzi who feed its cravings, and the World Wide Web all reinforce a cult of celebrity in which even the minutiae of private lives in a promiscuous range of occupations are accorded the status of news. Intrinsic to celebrity is the back-story, that biographical database that enables us to peer into each other's lives for a context in which to place the latest achievement, embarrassment or debacle.

Liszt was an artist who repeatedly reinvented himself: as a 'figure of omnipotence', a magician of sound and showmanship, master over pianos, women and audiences, Liszt knew a great deal about celebrity.[111] Taking his lead from Paganini, probably the first performer-composer to grasp the potential of celebrity in the cultural flux of post-Napoleonic Europe, Liszt adopted a series of tropes (the 'Napoleon of the piano', 'child of Paris',[112] German cultural protagonist, Hungarian nationalist) to optimise his impact on the musical world. In the same spirit, and by adapting the same strategy via a kind of literary osmosis, Liszt tried to ensure that Chopin would not remain intangible, that in death he would meet the public gaze that so repelled him in life by being transformed into a celebrity of the stricken heart.

In constructing his 'Chopin' Liszt drew upon a rich pedigree of biographical writing. In Roman times, Suetonius with his *On the Life of the Caesars*, a blend of archival research, eyewitness accounts and gossip, provided the model for historians of the principate to follow. During the Middle Ages evolved hagiography, a key Christian genre for teaching and worship with its template of *vita* (life), *acta* (deeds) and *passio* (martyrdom). It was not until the Renaissance that secular biography experienced its own rebirth at the hands of the painter Giorgio Vasari whose pioneering art-historical work *Lives of the Artists*

Introduction

(1550), a synthesis of research, anecdote and aesthetic judgement, featured the author himself as a sort of impresario. Partly in response to Vasari's work, literary biography then made great strides, not least with James Boswell's innovative *Life of Samuel Johnson* (1791) a work that, by exploring the private truth behind a public man, affirmed the vitality and importance of the genre in intellectual life.

Musicians' lives were not, however, deemed significant enough to be systematically documented until the mid-eighteenth century. Up to that time, music was regarded as an intrinsically contemporary, emphemeral form of entertainment, since, although there was an growing interest in 'ancient music', canon-formation lay in the future and there was no perceived need for musical biography, memoirs or autobiographies. First to appear were biographical dictionaries, a genre pioneered by Johann Mattheson whose lexicon of the 'best musicians' of the age, largely compiled from material supplied by the subjects themselves, had as its subtext the enhancement of musicians' place in society.[113] Within a century this genre had culminated in François Joseph Fétis's *Biographie universelle des musiciens* (1835–44), a 'landmark in musicology' which, by privileging the musical past over the progressivism of the present had, in effect, laid down a formidable challenge to Liszt's musical ideology.[114]

Composer monographs began to appear after 1800 and were in most cases characterised by authors' personal acquaintance, or family connection, with their subjects. By the time Liszt began work on *Chopin*, only a handful of major 'lives' had been published, among them those of J. S. Bach (Forkel, 1802), Rossini (Stendahl, 1824), Mozart (von Nissen, 1828) and Beethoven (Schindler, 1840), of which only Stendahl's *Vie* lacked a personal connection with its subject.[115] It is difficult to believe that Liszt was not familiar with them all.

Although Liszt left no clues as to what he drew from existing musical biographies, it is nevertheless useful to speculate as to what he *may* have absorbed from them. Forkel's *Bach*, a seminal source compiled with the assistance of two of the composer's sons, left a complex legacy. Written with the intention of retrieving its subject from obscurity, it provided a template of biography as 'rescue', opening the possibility that the biographer could make the dead and their music 'live' – and in a different way. By emphasising Bach's industry and learning, artistic courage and humanity, Forkel's work drew attention to the importance of feelings, the personality within, in any discussion of musical works. Perhaps above all from Liszt's point of view, Forkel gave musical biography a political dimension. By presenting Bach as a hero of German culture, Forkel pitched him headlong into the ferment of nationalist politics in Germany; as his closing exhortation declares: 'Let his country be proud of him; let it be proud, but, at the same time, worthy of him'.[116]

Surely Liszt also drew on Anton Schindler's *Life of Beethoven* (1840) which, despite its inaccuracies and falsifications, was the *ur-text* that constructed the nineteenth century's view of its subject.[117] With his credentials as biographer resting on his relationship with the composer, Schindler claimed that his approach was faithful to Beethoven's own admonition that future biographers should 'tell the truth about everything'.[118] In the process he portrayed Beethoven as worn down by a life of 'bitter sorrows' and 'deep injuries', an artist whose wilfulness and eccentricities resulted in an alienation of self and the resulting neglect by others.[119] In his frustrations, Schindler argues, Beethoven became a victim of his own creativity and love for truth, thereby acquiring a heroic grandeur, even a kind of counter-cultural celebrity.[120] In the same spirit, in *Chopin* Liszt not only makes much of the subject's suffering but also foregrounds the testimony of others to support his core biographical narrative. Like Schindler too, he emphasises his personal connection with, and intimate knowledge of, his subject, but goes further in that he claims to know Chopin's art from the inside. As he explained:

> In thinking of our long friendship with Chopin and of the admiration we held for him from his entry into the musical world, we recall that . . . we have been the frequent interpreter of his inspirations and, we boldly claim, the interpreter he loved and favoured the most. We, more often than others, received from his lips insight into the intricacies of his techniques, and that we, as an interpreter, were identified with his thoughts on his art and with the feelings he confided to it. (137)

Liszt seems also to have been influenced by the work of Stendahl, the French novelist and critic whose *Vie de Rossini* took musical biography decisively in a populist direction.[121] A groundbreaking work of music history and critical scholarship, Stendahl's *Vie* was written (as the preface proclaimed) to celebrate a 'Napoleon' of music, a revolutionary 'hero' whose 'throne of glory' was assured with operas that celebrated *la promesse de bonheur*.[122] Alongside its hagiographic elements it offered hard-hitting criticism of Rossini's operas while incorporating digressions on the cultural milieux of the age. With it

Introduction

Stendahl showed that musical biography could move out of the confines of scholarly discourse and be made appealing to a broad public. Perhaps too his work inspired Liszt to expand the possibilities of biography to incorporate digressive sweep and literary panache as well as defiant polemics.

Yet Liszt looked beyond previous biographers towards a more theoretical discourse in *Chopin*. He almost certainly (and probably like Schindler) drew on the work of the Belgian critic August Gathy, whose ideas enjoyed a vogue in the 1830 and 40s.[123] Gathy, who defined genius as the ability to create the original and give it form, posited that, since genius was by definition at the leading edge of artistic development, it had to wait for recognition. It followed that the adjuncts to genius were neglect, rejection and suffering, the true artist being doomed by his or her originality to be 'tragic'. It has been suggested that the heightened interest shown in Beethoven in the 1830s and 1840s may partly at least be ascribed to the influence of Gathy's ideas. Among living musicians, Berlioz was surely one of the first to identify with Gathy's image of the artist, pouring his manifold professional frustrations and disappointments into *Benvenuto Cellini* (1838), an opera that celebrated the triumph of the unorthodox, embattled artist over his enemies.

With *Chopin* Liszt went far beyond previous musical 'lives' in his radical attempt to reveal the 'true' Chopin to his readers. He gave his subject a contextual background that included notions of nation, class, nationalist politics, gender and even details of intimate relationships. Liszt fused scholarly and populist elements, seizing upon the potential of novelistic features to give his biography an expanded template. Of hardly less importance was that *Chopin* was also the first music biography to explore in pitiless detail the links between a composer's state of mind and his creative impulse. Anticipating Freud (and 'psychohistory') by half a century, Liszt attempted a psychoanalytical approach by 'constructing' Chopin's psychic reality – celebrity as psychological subject. In so doing, his work uncannily anticipates the late twentieth-century definition of the genre: 'What is distinctive about psychobiography as a scholarly enterprise is that the biographer is attempting to make some sense out of the subject's life course, or key phases in it, in terms of a consciously thought-out psychological interpretation of that subject's personality'.[124]

Perhaps it is not too fanciful to suggest that in *Chopin* Liszt was striving for what might be termed a 'biography of the future'. Certainly

Introduction

few biographers of the nineteenth century attempted anything as daring or original.

Liszt, one of the first and surely one of the most influential of musical biographers, adopted the discourse of celebrity to achieve his ends. Like a latter-day paparazzo, he ruthlessly sought to find a way into the most secret, and most private, recesses of his subject's life. And once he had succeeded, he carefully selected that which suited his turn. The peculiar paradox of *Chopin* is that it was intended not only as a sincere tribute to, and eternal vindication, of its subject but also as an exposé, at once controversial and merciless. Liszt well understood the commercial value of notoriety and how it could be made to serve the immortal values of art. More acutely than most musicians of his time, he understood that the semantic ambiguity of music, the wordlessness of many of its forms, needed historical textuality to establish musical meaning. His was the first life of the composer to be published and it was destined to remain for decades the only major study. It had the cachet of Liszt's celebrity and the authority of his exceptional personal links with its subject. For these and the many other reasons explored above, it immediately entered the bloodstream of music history.

Yet beyond its political contexts and cultural sub-texts we ignore at our peril that Liszt's stated aim in *Chopin* was to provide a fitting and lasting tribute to an erstwhile friend and comrade. There is a sense too in which Liszt sought to rescue Chopin from the mourners who had thronged the Madeleine on that October day; from the protective inner circle, the dour exiles, the wealthy patrons and pupils and, perhaps above all, from the curious yet largely indifferent general public. Years later, Liszt restated his particular contempt for members of the *beau monde* who had attended the funeral in such numbers: 'His [Chopin's] soul was not in the least affected by them [Parisian salons] and his work as an artist remains transparent, marvellous, ethereal, and of an incomparable genius – far removed from the errors of a school and the twitterings of a salon'.[125]

Chopin unquestionably has flaws. In places it is inaccurate, digressive and even bizarre, its co-authorship pulling the text in different directions. Liszt himself was aware of its shortcomings. Most music historians have dismissed it as irredeemably flawed, thereby overlooking its ambition, significance and many beauties. With its multiple agendas, at its heart it is an act of appropriation, a cultural and political polemic, a thoroughly Lisztian production: experimental,

Introduction

passionate, quirky and daring. Flaunting its author's celebrity, it is perhaps one of Liszt's most daring improvisations, and one with which he broke new ground in reaching out to the expanding music public of his time.

NOTES

1 Chopin's observation (in 1842) on his relationship with Liszt, as reported by his pupil Wilhelm von Lenz (1809–83) to Frederick Niecks. F. Niecks: *Frederick Chopin: As a Man and Musician* (Novello and Ewer, 1888), vol. ii, p. 171. The full citation reads: '[Chopin] defined his relations with Liszt thus: "We are friends, we were comrades". What he meant by the first half of the statement was no doubt: "Now we meet on only terms of only polite acquaintance".'
2 James W. Davison: *Musical World*, 10 November 1849, vol. xxiv, No. 45 pp. 705–6.
3 Hector Berlioz to his sister, Nanci Pal, 29 [sic] October 1849. Hugh Macdonald (ed.) / R. Nicols (trans.): *Berlioz: Selected Letters* (Faber and Faber, 1995), pp. 265–6.
4 Benita Eisler: *Chopin's Funeral* (Abacus Books, 2004) p. 10. The cost of the funeral in 2010 prices would be £280,000 according to the National Archives currency converter website. Jane Stirling (1804–59), one of Chopin's pupils and dedicatee of the *Nocturnes* Op. 55 (1844), was rumoured to want to marry him. Niecks: *Frederick Chopin*, vol. ii, pp. 291–2.
5 Chopin's income had so declined by 1849 that Jane Stirling offered him a gift of 25,000 francs – of which he accepted 15,000 fr. as a loan to cover his rent and daily needs. Eisler: *Chopin's Funeral*, pp. 211–12. That Chopin charged his pupils 20 francs per lesson in his heyday as a teacher puts the state of his finances (and Stirling's generosity) into perspective. Ibid. p. 119.
6 *Musical World*, 10 November 1849.
7 Adrian Williams: *Franz Liszt: Selected Letters* (Oxford: Oxford University Press, 1998), p. 282, n.4.
8 Karolyna Elizabeth von Sayn-Wittgenstein, née Iwanowska (1819–87), a devout Roman Catholic, was separated from her husband, a prince of German extraction by whom she had a daughter, when she met Liszt at a concert in Kiev. During a subsequent sojourn at Woronince, the princess's vast estate, the couple began a liaison and began making plans for a future together.
9 Liszt quoted in ibid., p. 130.
10 J. Samson: *Chopin* (Oxford: Oxford University Press, Master Musicians series, 1996), p. 69. See also, Halina Goldberg: *Music in Chopin's Warsaw* (Oxford: Oxford University Press, 2008).

Introduction

11 Letter: Chopin to Tytus Woyciechowski, 25 Dec. 1831. H. Opieński / E.L. Voynich (ed./tr.): *Chopin's Letters* (New York: Dover 1988), p. 166. See also Samson: *Chopin*, p. 65.
12 Z. Chechlińska: 'Chopin's Reception as Reflected in Nineteenth-Century Polish Periodicals: General Remarks', in H. Goldberg (ed.): *The Age of Chopin: Interdisciplinary Inquiries* (Bloomington: Indiana University Press, 2004), p. 248.
13 The partitions (of 1772, 1793 and 1795) had split Poland into three political zones: Russian, Austrian (Galicia), Prussian; it is noteworthy that Chopin's father took part in the abortive 'Kościuszko' uprising that resulted in the third partition.
14 Samson: *Chopin*, pp. 33 and 73; also W. G. Atwood: *Fryderyk Chopin: Pianist from Warsaw* (New York: Columbia University Press, 1987), p. 34.
15 Letter: Chopin to Matuszyński (1 Jan 1831), quoted in M. Karasowski / E. Hill (tr.): *Chopin: His Life, Letters and Works*, vol. i, pp. 190–2.
16 Prince Adam Jerzy Czartoryski (1770–1861), Polish statesman, was the leader of the conservative constitutionalists working for Polish independence.
17 The 'Carlists' supported the deposed reactionary Charles X, while the 'Philippists' backed the new 'bourgeois monarch', Louis-Philippe. Letter: Chopin to Dominik Dziewanowski (undated 1832) in Opieński / Voynich (ed./tr.): *Chopin's Letters*, p. 169.
18 For Liszt's relationship with Claude Henri, Comte de Saint-Simon, see A. Walker: *Franz Liszt: The Virtuoso Years 1811–47* (Faber and Faber, revised edition 1988), pp. 152–4.
19 Letters: Chopin to Józef Elsner, 14 Dec 1831, quoted in Karasowski / Hill (tr.): *Chopin: His Life, Letters and Works*, vol. ii, p. 227; and Chopin to Tytus Woyciechowski, (6 Dec. 1831), quoted p. 232.
20 Quoted in A. Walker: *Franz Liszt: The Final Years 1861–86* (Ithaca: Cornell University Press, 1996), vol. iii, p. 455.
21 This essay, entitled 'Sur la situation des artistes et leur condition dans la société', was published as a series of six articles in the *Gazette musicale* (1835). For the text see J. Chantavoine (ed.): *Pages romantiques* (Paris: Alcan, 1912), pp. 1–83.
22 The woman involved was the concert pianist Marie Pleyel, née Moke (1811–75), the dedicatee of Chopin's *Nocturnes* Op. 9 (1832).
23 Marie, Comtesse d'Agoult, née de Flavigny (1805–76), was married to a scion of one of France's oldest aristocratic families (by whom she had two children) when she met Liszt in 1833.
24 George Sand, born Aurore Dupin (1804–76), was already one of the most celebrated writers of the day, and a mother of two, when she met Chopin.

Introduction

25 Letter: Liszt to George Sand, 15 Dec. 1837. Williams: *Liszt: Letters*, p. 76.
26 Matters plumbed new depths when Sand portrayed d'Agoult as a monster of artifice in her own novel *Horace* (1841).
27 Niecks: *Frederick Chopin*, vol. ii, pp. 171.
28 For a detailed account of Liszt's return to his homeland see Walker: *Liszt: Virtuoso Years*, pp. 319–26.
29 Ibid., p. 335, n.37.
30 As, for example, in the *Fantasie romantique sur deux mélodies suisse* (1836), and the *Rondeau fantastique sur un thème espagnol 'El contrabandista'* (1836), a work dedicated to George Sand.
31 Quoted W. G. Atwood: *The Parisian Worlds of Frédéric Chopin* (New Haven: Yale University Press, 1999), p. 63. Adam Mickiewicz (1798–1855) was a nationalist, political radical, poet and visionary. For an exploration of the connection between Chopin's political and patriotic attitudes and Mickiewicz's work, see H. Goldberg: '"Remembering that tale of grief": the Prophetic Voice in Chopin's Music', in H. Goldberg (ed.): *The Age of Chopin*, pp. 56–63.
32 Atwood: *Parisian Worlds of Frédéric Chopin*, p. 63. Juliusz Słowacki (1809–49), poet, dramatist and exiled revolutionary, was a leading light among Polish Romantics.
33 Quoted in K. Wolff (ed.) / P. Rosenfeld (trans.): *Robert Schumann: On Music and Musicians* (Dobson, 1947), p. 132.
34 H. Goldberg: '"Remembering that tale of grief"', pp. 54–92. J. Kallberg: 'Hearing Poland: Chopin and Nationalism', in R. Larry Todd (ed.): *Nineteenth Century Piano Music* (Routledge, second edition 2004), pp. 221–57. J. Pekacs: 'The Nation's Property: Chopin's Biography as Cultural Discourse', in *Musical Biography: Towards New Paradigms* (Aldershot: Ashgate, 2006), pp. 43–68.
35 Translated from E. Legouvé: *Soixante ans de souvenirs* (Paris: Hetzel, 1886), vol. i, p. 309.
36 For a translation of Liszt's review, see Atwood: *Fryderyk Chopin: Pianist from Warsaw*, pp. 231–4. All the quotations from Liszt's article are from this source.
37 Letter: Chopin to Julian Fontana, 13 Sep. 1841 Opieński / Voynich (ed./tr): *Chopin's Letters*, p. 237.
38 Letter: Chopin to Fontana, 16 Aug. 1841, ibid., p. 232.
39 Niecks: *Frederick Chopin*, vol. ii, p. 113.
40 Letter: Liszt to Chopin, 26 Feb. 1843, Williams: *Liszt: Letters*, p. 195.
41 Eisler: *Chopin's Funeral*, pp. 138–9.
42 Letter: Liszt to Marie d'Agoult, 1 May 1847, Williams: *Liszt: Letters*, p. 249.
43 Letter: Liszt to Ludwika Jędrzejewiczowa (14 November 1849). For the full text of both letter and questionnaire, see M. Karlowicz: *Souvenirs inédits de Frédéric Chopin* (Paris: Welter, 1904), pp. 200–3.

Introduction

44 Walker: *Liszt: Virtuoso Years*, pp. 185–6. For an account of events surrounding Liszt's plans for the biography and the questionnaire, see also I. Poniatowska: 'The Polish Reception of Chopin's Biography by Franz Liszt', in H. Goldberg (ed.): *The Age of Chopin*, pp. 259–65.
45 I. Deák: *Lawful Revolution: Louis Kossuth and the Hungarians, 1848–1849* (New York: Columbia University Press, 1979), pp. 334–5.
46 *The Times*, 17 Oct. 1849. Haynau attracted such international opprobrium that on a visit to London the following year he was dragged from his carriage, beaten and almost thrown into the Thames by workers from a riverside brewery. Deák: *Lawful Revolution*, p. 302.
47 The work appeared in *Harmonies poétiques et religieuses* (S173, 1845–52), a set of piano pieces dedicated to Carolyne von Sayn-Wittgenstein.
48 'We are fully aware that in the portions of the work relating to Chopin's youth, manners, compositions, and to the Polish national music, Liszt received help from a Polish emigrant, Franz [sic] Grzymała'. Karasowski / Hill (tr.) *Chopin: His Life, Letters and Works*, vol. i, p. 38. Wojciech Grzymała (1793–1870), writer, soldier and financial speculator, was 'almost a father figure' in Chopin's life. Samson: *Chopin*, p. 307.
49 Letter: Liszt to Breitkopf und Härtel, 14 Jan, 1850 A. Walker: *Liszt: The Weimar Years 1848–61* (Ithaca: Cornell University Press, 1993, p. 374.
50 Letter: Charles Auguste de Sainte-Beuve to Liszt, 31 March 1850, quoted in S. Bernstein: *Virtuosity of the Nineteenth Century: Performing Music and Language in Heine, Liszt and Baudelaire* (Stanford: Stanford University Press, 1998), pp. 123–4.
51 Letter: Liszt to d'Ortigue, 24 Apr. 1850, in which Liszt thanked the critic for his warm response: 'The kind judgement you pass on three-quarters of my work gives me the most flattering encouragement, and I thank you very cordially for your observations on the fourth quarter, of which I shall not fail to take advantage'. Williams: *Liszt: Letters*, pp. 282–3.
52 During that summer, Liszt premièred Schumann's *Genoveva*, Wagner's *Lohengrin*, and his own *Prometheus* overture and choruses at Weimar. Also, in the autumn, the Princess fell worryingly ill.
53 M. Eckhardt, 'New Documents on Liszt as Author', *New Hungarian Quarterly* (Autumn 1984), pp. 181–94: p. 190.
54 Johann Gottfried Herder (1744–1803), pastor, philosopher and collector of folklore and folk poetry *Volkslied* had relatively little to say on the subject of folk music. See also S. Sadie (ed.): *The New Grove Dictionary of Music and Musicians* (second edition, Macmillan, 2001), entry on 'Nationalism' Part 4: 'Cultural Nationalism and German Nationalism' (vol. xvii, pp. 689–94), and Part 6: 'Music and German Nation-Building, the Vormärz Phase' (pp. 693–4, both R. Taruskin).
55 B. Anderson: *Imagined Communities: Reflections on the Origin and Spread of Nationalism*, revised edition (Verso, 2006), pp. 67–82.

Introduction

56 Only in a handful of countries (like Poland and Hungary) did liberal middle-class nationalism join forces with mass 'popular' nationalism. See M. Broers: *Europe after Napoleon: Revolution, Reaction and Romanticism, 1815–48* (Manchester: Manchester University Press, 1996), pp. 101–4.

57 A. Walicki: *Philosophy and Romantic Nationalism: The Case of Poland* (Notre Dame: University of Notre Dame Press, 1994), p. 28.

58 It has been estimated that about ten thousand individuals, mostly from the political, military and intellectual elite, left Poland. Walicki: *Philosophy and Romantic Nationalism*, p. 31.

59 See Walicki: pp. 241–5 and passim.

60 R. Gildea: *Barricades and Borders: Europe 1800–1914* (Oxford: Oxford University Press, second edition, 2003), pp. 72–3.

61 Quoted in Walker: *Liszt: Virtuoso Years*, p. 325.

62 That biographers have neglected Herder's influence on Liszt is puzzling, especially since Liszt aligned himself with German nationalist sentiment in the 1840s. Dana Gooley: *The Virtuoso Liszt* (Cambridge: Cambridge University Press, 2004), pp. 156–200 passim.

63 During the revolutionary turmoil in Vienna Liszt toured the rebel lines wearing Hungarian national colours and composed a chorus encouraging the working class (*Arbeiterchor*) – but declined to publish it for fear of inflaming the situation. Walker: *Liszt: Weimar Years*, pp. 68–71.

64 Liszt personally antagonised the Tsar over his nationalist views and Polish sympathies during his two Russian tours (1842–43). Walker: *Liszt: Virtuoso Years*, pp. 374–9. Relations with the Tsarist regime deteriorated further after the Princess von Sayn-Wittgenstein was officially exiled and her Russian lands sequestered (in the 1850s). Ibid., pp. 140–4.

65 Letter: Liszt to Carolyne von Sayn-Wittgenstein, 25 Apr. 1875, Williams: *Liszt: Letters*, pp. 783–4. Liszt's commitment to the Polish national cause never dimmed; as late as 1875, he began work on an oratorio on the life of St Stanislaus, the patron saint of Poland.

66 For Chopin and Polishness see Maja Trochimczyk's essay, 'Chopin and the "Polish Race": on National Ideologies and the Chopin Reception', in Goldberg (ed.): *The Age of Chopin*, pp. 278–313.

67 Ibid., p. 280.

68 Among the earliest antiquarian collectors of national music were Edward Jones with *Musical and Poetical Relicks of the Welsh Bards* (1784–1820); Patrick Macdonald with *Collection of Highland Airs* (1784); and Nikolay Aleksandrovitch L'vov with *Sobranyie narodnïkh russkikh pesen e ikh golosami* (1790), an anthology of Russian folk airs.

69 For a discussion of music and Russian national conciousness, see Sadie (ed.): *New Grove Dictionary* entry on 'Nationalism' Part 9: 'The Other Empire' (vol. xvii, pp. 696–9, Taruskin). As Taruskin makes clear, Glinka

Introduction

used Russian folk melodies to propagandise for the Romanov status quo rather than to celebrate a new enhanced sense of the music of 'the people'.

70 L. Wolff: *Inventing Eastern Europe: The Map of Civilisation in the Mind of the Enlightenment* (Stanford: Stanford University Press, 1994), p. 238.
71 Ibid., p. 306.
72 Ibid., pp. 211–20.
73 Balzac / Crawford M. A. (trans.): *Cousin Bette* (Penguin 1965), p. 119.
74 Ibid., p. 230.
75 Walicki: *Philosophy and Romantic Nationalism*, pp. 13–14.
76 Letter: Liszt to the Grand Duke of Weimar, Carl Alexander, 23 May 1849, Williams: *Liszt: Letters*, p. 273. Just days before he wrote this letter, Liszt had sheltered the fleeing Wagner at the Altenburg before facilitating his escape to Switzerland. Walker: *Liszt: Weimar Years*, pp. 113–19.
77 See W. Weber: 'Wagner, Wagnerism and Musical Idealism', in W. Weber / D. C. Large (eds): *Wagnerism in European Culture and Politics* (Ithaca: Cornell University Press, 1984), pp. 60–1.
78 Liszt / C. Suttoni (tr.): *An Artist's Journey: lettres d'un bachelier ès musique, 1835–41* (Chicago: University of Chicago Press, 1989), pp. xi–xii.
79 Quoted in Walker: *Liszt: Weimar Years*, p. 70.
80 Much later in life Liszt again commemorated some of the 'martyrs' of the revolution in a cycle of piano pieces, *Historische ungarische Bildnisse* (Historical Hungarian Portraits) (1885).
81 Letter: Liszt to Joseph d'Ortigue, 24 Apr. 1850, Williams: *Liszt: Letters*, pp. 282–3.
82 Several scholars have tried to shed light on Liszt's literary collaborations: E. Haraszti, 'Franz Liszt: Author Despite Himself', *Musical Quarterly* (1947), vol. xxxiii, pp. 490–516; M. Eckhardt, 'New Documents on Liszt as Author', *New Hungarian Quarterly* (Autumn 1984), pp. 181–94 already cited; and C. Suttoni's 'Liszt as Author', in Liszt / Suttoni (ed.): *An Artist's Journey*, pp. 238–45. See also Walker: *Liszt: Virtuoso Years*, pp. 19–23.
83 Walker: *Liszt: Weimar Years*, pp. 376–9.
84 Quoted Ibid. The original manuscript has been lost except for a twenty-three-page fragment which disappeared into a private collection in the 1970s.
85 Eckhardt: 'New Documents on Liszt as Author', p. 182.
86 Letter: Liszt to Breitkopf and Härtel, 14 Jan. 1850, see Walker: *Liszt: Weimar Years*, p. 374.
87 Legouvé: *Soixante ans de souvenirs*, vol. i, p. 309.
88 Hippolyte Barbedette, writing a decade later, quotes the passage cited above verbatim. H. Barbedette: *Chopin: essai de critique musicale* (Paris: Leiber, 1861), p. 10.

Introduction

89 T. Dormandy: *The White Death: A History of Tuberculosis* (Hambledon, 1999), pp. 41–2.
90 'Bohemianism' reached its apogee with Henri Mürger's collection of short stories *Scènes de la vie de Bohême*, published in the 1840s.
91 See D. F. Krell: *Contagion: Sexuality, Disease and Death in German Idealism and Romanticism* (Bloomington: Indiana University Press, 1998), pp. 195–6.
92 Barbedette: *Chopin: essai de critique musicale*, p. 65.
93 P. Ariès: *Western Attitudes towards Death: From the Middle Ages to the Present* (Baltimore: Johns Hopkins University Press, 1974), pp. 57–61. It may be significant that the poet-politician Alphonse de Lamartine (1790–1869), one of the most powerful influences on Liszt's intellectual development, had a seminal role in the invention of the 'romantic death' with his *Méditations poétiques* (1820).
94 Letter: Liszt to Marie d'Agoult, 1 May 1847, Williams: *Liszt: Letters*, pp. 248–50. In this letter, Liszt boasted that Marie had fallen in love with him, quoting her as pleading: 'Take me, take me, anywhere you like; I shan't bother you. I can sleep all day; in the evening you can let me go to the theatre; and at night you can do with me what you will!'
95 J. J. McGann (ed.): *Lord Byron: Complete Poetical Works* (Oxford: Clarendon Press 1986), vol. iv, p. 23.
96 Quoted in Walker: *Liszt: Virtuoso Years*, p. 23.
97 Eckardt: 'New Documents on Liszt as Author', p. 189.
98 For the Princess's determination to expand upon Liszt's texts, see Walker: *Liszt: Weimar Years*, pp. 378, 388n, 389.
99 I am grateful to Dr Jean-Claude Pascal-Ferrer of the University of Bordeaux for his insights on Liszt's style, and for his comments on my translated text.
100 In the second edition (*nouvelle édition*), which appeared in 1879, the text had been bulked out with over a hundred pages and much of the material rearranged.
101 G. Sand: *Lucrezia Floriani* (1847, Paris: Michel Levy Frères 1867), p. 50. All quotations from Sand's novel are translated from Liszt's published text. The page references are taken from Sand's definitive edition as republished in 1867. For an English language edition of the novel, see G. Sand / Eker J. (tr.): *Lucrezia Floriani* (Chicago: Academy Chicago Publishers 1993).
102 The questionnaire that Liszt sent to Ludwika tends to support the view that he had only the sketchiest idea of Chopin's personal history.
103 Sand described Liszt in her diary (3 June 1837) as 'a powerful artist, sublime in the great things, always superior in the small ones, yet sad, and troubled by a secret wound', quoted in B. Jack: *George Sand* (Vintage, 2001), p. 271.

Introduction

104 Eisler: *Chopin's Funeral*, pp. 159–63. Eugène Delacroix (1798–1863), probably the most influential figure among French Romantic painters, was a close friend and confidant of Chopin.
105 Letter: Chopin to Gryzmała, 17–18 Nov. 1848, quoted in Niecks: *Frederick Chopin*, vol. ii, p. 304.
106 Samson: *Chopin*, p. 244.
107 Karasowski / Hill (tr.): *Chopin: His Life, Letters and Works*, vol. ii, p. 307.
108 Letter: Liszt to Carolyne von Sayn-Wittgenstein, 23 May 1847, Williams: *Liszt: Letters*, pp. 250–1. In another letter written to the Princess that same month Liszt reported in a more sober vein that: '*Lucrezia Floriani* is generally disliked. Talent has not adequately cloaked the vulgarity of the confession. It still seems that she [Sand] wants to leave Chopin from sheer boredom, and that he is hanging on'. Ibid., pp. 251–2.
109 Sand: *Lucrezia Floriani*, p. 4.
110 Joseph Bennett: *Frédéric Chopin* (Novello, c. 1899), pp. 4–5.
111 Gooley: *The Virtuoso Liszt*, p. 2.
112 Ibid., p. 122.
113 Johann Mattheson (1681–1764) published his *Grundlage einer Ehren-Pforte* in 1740. See entry 'J Mattheson', in S. Sadie (ed.), *New Grove Dictionary* (G. J. Buelow, vol. xvi, pp. 139–44). See also Hans Lenneberg: *Witnesses and Scholars: Studies in Musical Biography* (Gordon & Breach, 1988), pp. 18–37.
114 See entry on 'F.-J. Fétis' in S. Sadie (ed.), *New Grove Dictionary* (vol. viii, pp. 746–9, Katharine Ellis).
115 See ibid. for entries on 'J.-N. Forkel' (vol. ix, pp. 89–91, G. B. Stauffer); 'Stendahl' (vol. xxiv, pp. 348–350, J. Johnson); 'Georg von Nissen' (vol. xix, pp. 3–4, R. Angermüller / W.Stafford); 'A. Schindler' (vol. xxii, p. 510, K. M. Knittel). The first monograph on a 'historic' composer was G. Baini's biography of Palestrina (1828).
116 J. N. Forkel: 'On Johann Sebastian Bach's Life, Genius, and Works', in H. T. David / A. Mendel / C. Wolff (eds.): *The New Bach Reader* (New York: Norton, 1999), p. 479. To emphasise the political nature of his work Forkel subtitled his biography 'for the patriotic admirers of musical art'.
117 A. F. Schindler / I. Moscheles (ed./tr.): *The Life of Beethoven*, 2 vols (Colburn, 1841).
118 Ibid., vol. i, p. 12.
119 Ibid.
120 Ibid., vol. ii, p. 315.
121 Stendahl (1783–1842) (Henri Beyle) had published an earlier volume of musical biography, *Vies de Haydn, Mozart et Métastase* (1814), most of which was gleaned from the work of others. See, S. Sadie (ed.), *New Grove Dictionary* entry 'Stendahl' vol. xxiv, pp. 348–50, J. Johnson.
122 Stendahl / R. N. Coe (trans.): *The Life of Rossini* (Calder, 1985), p. 3.

Introduction

123 August Gathy (1800–58) was sometime Paris critic of the *Allgemeinen Zeitung* and *Neuen Musikalischer Zeitung*; see Lenneberg: *Witnesses and Scholars*, pp. 123–4.
124 R. C. Tucker quoted in W. M. Runyan: *Life Histories and Psychobiography: Explorations in Theory and Method* (Oxford: Oxford University Press, 1984), p. 201.
125 Liszt to Wilhelm von Lenz, 20 Sep. 1872, quoted in Williams: *Liszt Letters*, pp. 749–50.

1 Chopin c. 1849, photograph by L. A. Bisson

2 Église Sainte Marie-Madeleine 'La Madeleine' c. 1855, Paris (VIII arrondissement), where Chopin's sumptuous funeral service was held on 30 October 1849

3 Princess Carolyne von Sayn-Wittgenstein c. 1847, daguerreotype, photographer unknown, Odessa (Ukraine)

4 George Sand c. 1840

5 Liszt c. 1858, photograph by Franz Hanfstaengl

6 The Altenburg, the house in Weimar where *Chopin* was written.
Photograph: Judy Rawlings

7 A facsimile of a manuscript page from Chapter 2 of *Chopin*

F. CHOPIN

PAR

F. LISZT.

PARIS
M. ESCUDIER, ÉDITEUR, RUE RICHELIEU, 102.
LEIPZIG, BRUXELLES,
BREITKOFF ET HARTEL. CHEZ SCHOTT.

1852

8 Title-page of the first edition of *Chopin*

CHAPTER 1

However much Chopin may be mourned by his fellow artists, as well as by those who knew him, we doubt whether the time has yet come for him, whose loss we feel so keenly, to hold the high rank that will probably be his in the future.[1]

If, as has often been proved, *no one is a prophet in his own homeland*, then is it not also the case that prophets, that is to say the men of the future who sense it and bring it closer in their works, remain unrecognised in their own times? Generations of young artists have protested in vain against reactionaries whose invariable custom is to strike at the living through the dead. It is time alone, in music as in the other arts, which can sometimes reveal true beauty and quality.

Since the many forms of art are only varied incantations designed to evoke feelings and passions so that they become intelligible and tangible, genius manifests itself in the invention of new art forms, adapted to feelings that have yet to be experienced even within the magic circle [of artists]. Surely it is already the case that in those arts in which sensation is combined with emotion without the intermediation of thought and reflection, the introduction of unfamiliar forms and styles is already an obstacle to the immediate understanding of a work? The surprise and fatigue caused by unfamiliar impressions make a work appear to many people as if written in an incomprehensible and barbaric language. The sheer effort of accustoming the ear to a work leads many stubbornly to refuse to study it. On the other hand, those with the greatest vitality and youthfulness, and those least enslaved by habit, are the first to be curious, and then passionate, about a new idiom. It is through them that the stubborn public will grasp the meaning, scope and construction of a new idiom and do justice to its riches. Thus musicians who do not confine themselves to the conventional need the help of time more than other artists. They cannot assume that death will give to their works that instant added value that it gives to paintings. No musician, to make his manuscripts more profitable, could repeat the deception practised by one of the great Flemish painters who, wishing to exploit his future glory, directed his wife to announce his death so that the canvases with which he had decorated his studio might increase in value.[2]

Whatever may be the current popularity of certain works by Chopin, a composer broken by suffering long before his death it is none the less probable that posterity will grant his works more than the shallow and flimsy esteem that has so far been awarded. Those who write the history of music will determine his status, but it will surely be a great one. With his rare melodic genius and remarkably expansive harmonic textures, his triumphs will rightly eclipse many works of greater length though they be played and replayed by large orchestras, or sung again and again by flocks of *prime donne*.

By restricting himself to the limited resources of the piano, Chopin, in our opinion, gave proof of one of the most essential qualities of any creative artist: the true appreciation of the medium in which he had the gifts to excel. Yet this fact, which we regard as a great strength, has proved prejudicial to his reputation. Any other composer, gifted with such harmonic and melodic powers, would surely have found it impossible to resist the temptations of the singing bow, the languor of the flute or the deafening power of the trumpet. What conviction was required for him to restrict himself to a field apparently so barren and through his genius make such ground fertile! What intuition is revealed by the decision to wrest certain instrumental effects from their usual domain and transfer them into a more limited, but far more idealised, sphere! What instinctive confidence in the future powers of his instrument governed the removal of such great thoughts from other, more usual, instruments! How we must admire his unique preoccupation with the beautiful for its own sake, a commitment that preserved his talent from the prevalent tendency to scatter scraps of melody over a hundred orchestral desks, and inspired him to expand the resources of art by teaching how to concentrate them within a smaller framework!

Far from aspiring to the uproar of the orchestra, Chopin was content to express his thoughts entirely on the ivory of the keyboard, achieving his goal without loss of power and without recourse to orchestral effects or to the scene-painter's broad brush. The value of his delicate pencil drawings has received too little serious attention. Today it is usual to regard as great only those composers who have written at least half a dozen operas, as many oratorios and a few symphonies, in response to the demand that they do everything – and a

Chapter 1

little more that everything. This generally held notion is however very problematical. While we do not dispute the hard-won glory or the real superiority of epic bards, whose creations are on such a large scale, we should like to apply to music the same value-system that is applied to material proportions in other branches of the fine arts. As, for example, in painting, where a canvas of twenty inches square, such as *La vision d'Ézéchiel*, or *Le cimetière* by Ruysdael, is placed among masterpieces and is more highly valued than a far larger picture, even though it might be by Rubens or Tintoretto.[3] In literature, is Béranger a lesser poet because he condensed his thoughts within the narrow limits of song?[4] Does not Petrarch owe his success to his sonnets, and yet how many who recite their exquisite rhymes are even aware of his epic on Africa?[5] We are sure that the prejudice, which still disputes the creative superiority of a composer of sonatas like those of Franz Schubert over another who merely serves up lifeless tunes in unmentionable operas, will gradually disappear. Likewise in music, in compositions of all kinds there will come an appreciation of eloquence and talent that express thoughts and feelings regardless of scale and interpretative means.

Any intelligent survey of Chopin's compositions will encounter beauties of a very high order, an entirely new expressiveness and a harmonic structure as original as it is learned. In his music boldness always justifies itself; richness, even exuberance, does not interfere with clarity; originality never degenerates into quirkiness; the sculpting is always orderly; and luxurious ornamentation never overloads the elegance of principal lines. His best works are full of effects that are epoch-making in the treatment of musical style: daring, brilliant and seductive they conceal their profundity beneath so much grace, their ingenuity beneath so much charm, that it is difficult to break their seductive appeal coolly to judge their theoretical, abstract value. Although the latter has been already been sensed, it will be increasingly recognised when the time comes for a thorough examination of the music of Chopin's era.

It is to Chopin that we owe the extension of chords, be they struck together, in arpeggio or spread; those chromatic and enharmonic lines, of which his music offers such striking examples; and those little groups of embellishing notes that fall like dewdrops upon the melody. He gave this type of ornament, which originated in the *fioritures* of the old school of Italian song, a surprise and variety beyond the range of the human voice which, until then, had been slavishly imitated by the piano in a stereotypical and monotonous manner. He also invented admirable harmonic progressions that gave a serious character even to pages that, because of the lightness of their subject, seemed to have no claim to any importance. Yet, what does the subject matter? Surely what matters is its gushing force, the pulsating emotion that intensifies, ennobles and magnifies it? What subtlety, above all what art, may be found in the masterpieces of La Fontaine, with their familiar subjects and innocuous titles![6] It is likewise with Chopin's études and préludes, pieces of no lesser perfection in genres he himself created, which sprang, like all his works, from his distinctive poetic genius. Written at the beginning of his career they are characterised by a youthful eloquence that fades in his more elaborate and contrived later works, and which disappears altogether from the last works with their overexcited sensibility and sense of exhaustion.

If we had to speak here in academic terms of the development of piano music, Chopin's works would yield a rich harvest for comment. First, we would explore his nocturnes, ballades, impromptus and scherzos that are filled with harmonic refinements as unfamiliar as they are unexpected, and then we would turn to his polonaises, mazurkas, waltzes and boleros. But this is neither the time nor the place for such a task, which would be of interest only to those knowledgeable in counterpoint and figured bass.

It is the feeling, highly romantic and individual, which suffuses these works that has made them widely known and popular. They are characteristic of the composer while being sympathetic not only to that country to which he brings honour but also to all those who are touched by the misfortune of exile and the tenderness of love.

Not always satisfied with the forms that he had evolved with such freedom, Chopin also wanted to frame his musical thought within classical limitations. Although he wrote beautiful concertos and sonatas, in these works it is clear that there is more determination than inspiration. When inspired his was an imperious, uncontrolled and impulsive talent. His style demanded freedom, and we believe that he abused his genius whenever he subjected it to rules, regulations and forms that were alien to his talent and which failed to accord with his instincts: he was an artist whose grace was best displayed when roaming freely.

Perhaps Chopin aspired to this double success by the example of his friend Mickiewicz? The latter, having endowed his language with imaginative poetry by founding a school of Slav literature with *Dziady*

Chapter 1

and his romantic ballads, then showed in *Grazyna* and *Wallenrod* that he could also conquer the stifling limitations of the classical tradition and prove himself the equal of the ancient poets.[7] In our opinion Chopin was unsuccessful in making a similar attempt since he could not sustain within an angular and rigid mould the floating and indefinite contour that is the charm of his musical thought. He was unable to restrict his hazy and shaded uncertainties which, smoothing all edges of form draped it in misty vapour, such as surrounded Ossian's beauties as they permitted mortals to glimpse their nubile outlines through the shifting clouds.[8]

Nevertheless, his works in classical genres glow with a rare dignity of style and have passages of great fascination and sections of surprising grandeur. We give as an example the Adagio of the *Second Concerto*, for which Chopin had a preference and which he liked to play frequently. The subordinate material is in his best manner and the principal phrase has an admirable breadth as it alternates with a recitative in setting the minor key as its antistrophe. The whole movement has an ideal perfection, its feeling by turns radiant and full of sympathy. It conjures up a magnificent landscape flooded with light, a happy Vale of Tempe as a backdrop to a melancholy scene of some sad tale.[9] It is as if an irreparable grief overwhelms the human heart in the middle of nature's splendour, a contrast sustained by a merging of tones and a softening of contrasts that prevents anything harsh from intruding upon the impression of joy tempered and sorrow comforted.

Neither can we ignore the Funeral March of the *First Sonata*, which was orchestrated after Chopin's death and first performed at his funeral.[10] What else could have expressed the sadness that accompanied to his last rest one who understood how great loss should be mourned? We once heard a young compatriot of his say: 'these pages could only have been written by a Pole'. Indeed, the funeral march of an entire nation, solemn and grief-stricken, weeping at its own demise, is to be found in this lament. The essence of mystical hope, a holy appeal to divine mercy, to infinite leniency, and to a justice that embraces every tomb and cradle – the exalted resignation of so many sorrows borne with heroism inspired by Christian martyrs – all resound in this song of grieving supplication. The music quivers indescribably with all that is most pure, holy, resigned, believing and hopeful in the hearts of women, children and priests. We feel it is not the death of a single warrior that is mourned, but rather the death of an entire generation. And yet this funereal and pitiful chant is of such penetrating sweetness that it does not seem of this world. These sounds, softened by distance, impose a profound meditation as if they were sung by angels around the divine throne. No cries, groans, blasphemies or imprecations disturb a lament that suggests the sighs of angels. The ancient face of grief is entirely absent; nothing recalls Cassandra's fury, Priam's humiliation, Hecuba's frenzy or the despair of the Trojan prisoners. The survivors of this Christian Troy have a superb faith that destroys the bitterness of suffering and the cowardice of despair. Their sorrow, no longer marked by earthly weakness, tears itself free from earth, moist with blood and tears, to fly towards God, and approach the Supreme Judge with prayers so poignant that our hearts, hearing them, break with dignified pity.

It would however be mistaken to believe that all of Chopin's compositions are limited to the mood of strenuous sacrifice and brave gentleness that is expressed in the sublime Funeral March. Muffled rage and suppressed anger are encountered in many passages of his works as, for example, in several of his études, and likewise in his scherzos, where a concentrated frustration dominated by a despair, sometimes ironic sometimes haughty, is depicted. That these dark outbursts have attracted less attention, and have been less understood, than his more tender poems is partly due to Chopin's personality: kind, affable, even-tempered and cheerful, he gave few outward signs of the secret convulsions that troubled him.

His character was not easy to fathom since, at first glance, it was made up of a thousand nuances that crossed and disguised each other in a bewildering way. It was easy to misjudge what he was really thinking, as is generally the case with Slavs whose loyalty and frankness, familiarity and a captivating ease of manner do not imply confidence or openness. Their feelings are kept half hidden, half-revealed, like the coils of an entwined serpent, and it is naive to take at face value their politeness or their outward humility. Their concepts of manners and modesty are rooted in customs that can be traced back to their historic connections with the Orient. Free of Muslim impassivity, they nevertheless learned from it a wary reserve in all delicate and private matters – so much so that when they speak of themselves they almost always exercise a reticence towards their questioner to gain an intellectual and emotional advantage. In conversation they often withhold judgemental contexts or motives, a ploy which they hide behind a subtle, questioning, derisive smile. Taking pleasure in mystification, from the most spiritual and comic to the most bitter and melancholy, with mocking deceit they assert a superiority which they inwardly feel but which they mask with the care and cunning of an oppressed people.

Chopin's frail and sickly constitution deterred him from the vigorous expression of his passions, so that even to his friends he revealed only a gentle and affectionate side. After all, in the hurried, distracted life of large cities, where no one has time to study the complex destinies of others and where everyone is judged by their public lives, few think it worthwhile to delve beneath the superficial. Yet those who became close to him would occasionally glimpse an impatience and irritation that his outward demeanour was taken so literally. And yet, in performance, the artist could not avenge the man! Too feeble in health to express his frustrations in his playing, he tried to compensate by composing music that he loved to hear performed with a vigour that he himself could not command. His works swirl with the passionate rancour of a man suffering from wounds more serious than he is prepared to acknowledge, just as shattered beams and spars swirl around a sinking ship.

These resentments were all the more important in Chopin's life because they so obviously manifested themselves in his music. Little by little they produced a state of unhealthy irritability which, reaching a point of febrile agitation produced the deformation, that twisting of thought, which is found in his final compositions. Almost suffocating and weighed down by repressed violence, in these works he uses art to speak to himself of his own tragedy. In the music published under these influences are found analogies with the convoluted emotions of Jean-Paul,[11] who needed surprises triggered by natural and physical phenomena, sensations of voluptuous terror stemming from unnatural occurrences and the morbid excitements of a hallucinating mind to move hearts already saturated with passion and indifferent to suffering. Likewise, a Chopin melody is sometimes so tormented, so nervous, so desperately persistent in its reworking of motifs, that it becomes as painful as watching the sufferings of body and soul where death is the only relief. Chopin was prey to a disease which, getting worse from year to year took him while still young – and in the music of which we speak may be found traces of the acute sufferings that devoured him, like the claw marks of a bird of prey on a beautiful body.

CHAPTER 2

CHOPIN'S EMOTIONAL ABERRATIONS, which never diminish the rare harmonic fabric of his music, and if anything make it more interesting to study, seldom occur in his best known and most enjoyed works. His polonaises, which are less familiar than they ought to be because of their technical difficulties, are among his highest inspirations. They never remind us of the affected, tricked-up *polonaises à la Pompadour* such as are promoted by ballroom orchestras and concert virtuosi and found in the hackneyed repertoire of insipid salon music.[1] His polonaises, characterised as they are by an energetic rhythm, surprise and electrify even the most lethargic and indifferent of listeners. The most noble and traditional feelings of historic Poland are embedded in them, and they express the resolve and gravity of its great men of the past. Generally martial in character, they portray courage with a simple directness that is the distinctive trait of this warlike nation. They breathe a calm and reflective power that recalls the Poles as they are depicted in their chronicles: strongly built, quick witted, deeply devout and indomitably courageous, and possessed of a courtesy and gallantry that never deserted them in time of war. Despite the domestic and legal limitations which their customs (resembling those of their neighbours and enemies the Turks) imposed upon their women, their inherent gallantry nevertheless glorified and immortalised queens who became saints, vassals who became queens, and beautiful subjects for whose sake thrones were imperilled or lost. Poland's history has its own terrible Sforza, scheming d'Arquien and flirtatious Gonzaga.[2]

With the Poles of former times the blend of masculine resolve with devotion to the women they loved could become strangely compulsive, noble to the point of pomposity. A good example of this characteristic may be found in the tender and devoted letters that Jan Sobieski wrote daily to his wife, missives dictated while facing Turkish battle standards that were as numerous as the ears of grain in a field.[3] The Poles acquired their taste for stateliness from observing the finest types of solemn ceremonial among the followers of Islam, whose qualities they appreciated and appropriated even while repelling their invasions. Like them, the Poles did not act without careful deliberation, keeping in mind the motto of Prince Bolleslas of Pomerania: 'first weigh it; then dare' (*Erst wieg's, dann wag's*).[4] Consequently, their impulse had a stately pride, leaving them with an ease and freedom of spirit that was open to the slightest show of tender care, to the most transient fears of the heart and to the most trivial matters in life. As they proudly valued life, so they knew how to beautify it and, better still, how to love and revere what made it beautiful and precious.

The chivalric heroism of the Poles was supported by an arrogant dignity, but, since calculation and reason underpinned their moral virtue, they succeeded in winning the admiration of people throughout their history – even that of their enemies. It was this sort of reckless wisdom, with its daring caution and fanatic fatalism that characterised the expedition of Sobieski when he saved Vienna and delivered a mortal blow to the Ottoman Empire. Thereby, the Turks were conquered at last, after a long struggle that was waged on both sides with prowess and a mutual respect between enemies as irreconcilable in war as they were magnanimous in times of truce.

While listening to some of Chopin's polonaises, one can imagine hearing the steady, heavy tread, of soldiers facing with brave pride all the injustices of fate. At times, they seem to have the same power as Paolo Veronese's magnificent group portraits,[5] as the imagination clothes these formations in the rich costumes of another age. Gold brocades, velvets, floral satins and soft flowing sables; sleeves casually tossed over the shoulder; inlaid sabres and boots of yellow or gold; tight blouses, pearl-encrusted bodices, headdresses glittering with rubies or emeralds, slippers embroidered with amber and gloves perfumed with the scent of a harem. These formations stand out from the dim background of a vanished time, surrounded by sumptuous Persian carpets and filigreed furniture from Constantinople, decorated with the extravagance of magnates who drank Tokay from embossed goblets. Those same grandees that shod their Arabian horses with silver and surmounted their escutcheons with the same elective crown that they hoped to gain, and which they wore as a symbol of their glorious equality of rank.[6]

According to those who saw the polonaise performed at the beginning of this century, it has so degenerated that now it is difficult to grasp its original character. Its decline began, alongside that of other national dances, at the time when the appropriate national costume fell out of use. This was especially true of the polonaise, which was stripped of rapid movement, its intricately choreographed steps and demanding poses. Since it evolved more for display than for seduction, the polonaise lost its meaning as a spectacle as soon as the men were deprived of the accessories essential for gestures of play and pantomime which brought alive its simple pattern. Today it is a circulating promenade, dull and of little interest, its many spontaneous improvised incidents and expressive mimicry impossible to imagine without the testimony of those elderly Poles who still wear traditional national dress. Most unusually, the polonaise was intended to draw attention to men, to emphasise their looks, courtly manner and military bearing. (Does not 'military and courtly' define the Polish character?) It is no coincidence that the name of the dance was a masculine noun mistakenly translated into the feminine.

Those who have never worn the *kontusz*,[7] a kind of kaftan that invited the wearer to toss back the sleeves, would find it difficult to imagine the mannerisms, slow bows, sudden straightening and subtleties of silent pantomime which the Poles of times past displayed as they paraded military-fashion in the polonaise. As they did so, the men fingered their long moustaches or their sword-hilts, both integral parts of the costume and objects of vanity for all. Diamonds and sapphires often sparkled upon weapons suspended from belts of cashmere or from silk sashes embroidered with gold, setting off frames that were always rather corpulent. Often the moustache veiled, without concealing, some scar, which made a greater impact than the most precious stones. Since luxurious materials, jewels and bright colours were as prevalent among the men as among the women, these stones were found (as with Hungarian costume)[8] in the buttons, rings, clasps, and plumes and aigrettes on brilliant velvet caps. During the dance, it was considered an art in itself to know how to doff and don, and otherwise manipulate the cap, movements especially remarked upon since the cavalier of the leading couple, as leader of the file, gave the word of command for the rest of the train.

In a Polish nobleman's house the host always opened a ball by leading off in a polonaise, his partner being neither the youngest nor the most beautiful but the most socially distinguished lady present. The most eminent guests came next, having chosen their partners out of friendship, or hope of advancement, and followed closely in his steps. The host's task was to lead the formation in a thousand

Chapter 2

capricious meanderings through apartments thronged with guests who were later to join the brilliant procession. Although the dancers liked to be conducted through the most distant galleries, gardens and groves, where only distant echoes of the music reached the ear, they welcomed the return to the ballroom where they were always greeted with redoubled fanfares. The spectators, constantly shifting and arranged like hedgerows along the route, observed the host's every movement, while he for his part combined in his bearing that male dignity tempered with gaiety that won him the admiration of the women and the jealousy of the men. Both vain and joyful, the host, with touching innocence, conveyed to his guests the pride he felt in being surrounded by such distinguished friends and eminent supporters who were there to render him honour.

Guided by the host in the first circuit, the dancers were led through long detours, where they encountered architectural and decorative surprises in keeping with the pleasures of the day and which the host would display with pride. The more imaginative and unexpected the artifice, the more the younger guests applauded, the more noisy were the compliments, the more joyous the laughter and the more the host would gain in reputation and be sought after as a partner. If he were of a certain age, he would receive, upon his return from one of these circuits, a deputation of young women who thanked and congratulated him on behalf of everyone. These pretty promenaders increased the curiosity of the other guests and served to heighten the sense of expectation for the polonaises that were to follow.

In this land of aristocratic democracy [*ce pays d'aristocratique démocratie*], at every ball there were those assembled in the galleries, all noble, and including many dependants of great aristocratic houses, who had voluntarily abstained from the festivities because they felt themselves too poor to join in. However, because it was felt no less important to impress them too, the sumptuously elegant band, shedding iridescent light, like a long serpent with glittering rings, first uncoiled its full length for them, displaying its brilliant sinuous outline. Like muffled bells came the sound of golden chains, the rustling of heavy and gorgeous damasks, of trailing sabres; and like a merry hiss came murmuring of voices from afar that, coming closer, became more like the sound of a sparkling river.

How could the genius of hospitality which, in Poland, drew its inspiration as much from the refinements of advanced civilisation as from the simplicity and innate courtesy of peasant manners, be absent from the polonaise? After the host had honoured his guests by inaugurating the ball, every male guest had the right to partner the host's lady. Clapping his hands to halt the procession, the guest bowed to the lady and asked her to accept the change, while the host did the same to the lady next in the line, the whole train following suit. The ladies, changing partners whenever a new cavalier claimed the honour of leading the one first chosen by the host, remained in the same order throughout the polonaise, while the gentlemen continually replaced each other. Thus the host, who had commenced the dance, might find himself last, or even completely excluded, before its close.

Every cavalier who, in turn, headed the column tried to surpass his predecessor in the originality and the complexity with which he led the dancers. He revealed his art as well as his right to lead with tight, complex and imaginative figures, executing them with such accuracy and conviction that the living ribbon twisted in every direction but never frayed in confusion or collision. As for the rest of the column, it only had to maintain the gait set and not to lag behind. The step, being rhythmic and swaying, gave the whole body a harmonious swing so that the dancers glided like swans on a river, their waists moving with the undulations of imperceptible waves. The gentleman would offer his lady now one hand then the other; sometimes touching only the points of her fingers, sometimes clasping her whole hand in his own. Never leaving her, he would circle to her right, then to her left and as each couple copied these movements they rippled through the entire length of the huge snake. Although apparently absorbed by these many manoeuvres, the cavalier still found time to bend to his lady and whisper to her compliments if she were young; if not young, then confidences, requests or snippets of news. Then, proudly straightening, he made his steely weapons ring, stroked, his thick moustache, and became so expressive in gesture that the lady felt obliged to give a sympathetic response.

Thus, in its original form the polonaise was no commonplace or meaningless promenade, but rather a procession in which an entire society was splendidly displayed, and in which it admired its own beauty, nobility, sumptuousness and courtesy. Men grown grey in military service or in oratory; captains who wore armour more often than the robes of peace; high-ranking clergymen; dignitaries of state; aged senators; warlike palatines; and ambitious castellans: these were the dancers most sought after by the youngest and most

Chapter 2

brilliant ladies present. Honour and honours made all ages equal and gave an advantage even over love itself. When we were told of the forgotten complexity and vanished relevance of this majestic dance by those who would never abandon the ancient *zupan*[9] and *kontusz* and still wore (like their ancestors) their hair closely cut round their temples, we understood this proud nation's ingrained instinct for display.

When we visited Chopin's homeland, his memory constantly guiding and stimulating our interest, we were fortunate to meet several of those individuals who are daily becoming rarer; because European civilisation, although it does not alter the fundamental basis of national characteristics, erases and refines their rough edges and outward forms. Although some of these men were of a superior intelligence, cultivated, erudite and strongly defined by a life of action, their horizons did not extend beyond the boundaries of their land, society, literature and traditions. In our discussions with them (facilitated by an interpreter) we glimpsed from their attitude towards new ways and customs what had contributed to their greatness, charm and weakness in the past. It was curious to encounter the inimitable originality of their utterly exclusive point of view. By limiting their opinions upon many subjects, their outlook gave them a peculiar strength, a concentrated energy and a keen and wild intuition, in pursuing their goals and cherished interests. Their mentality regarded everything beyond an immediate purpose as foreign and yet, it alone, like a faithful mirror, provided a panorama of the past, preserving its true aspect and vivid setting: it alone reflected the disappearance of ways and customs and the spirit that created them.

Chopin was born too late and left home too early to possess this same spirit. Yet in childhood he knew many who did, and from these memories he absorbed the secrets of its ancient glories – which he rescued from neglect, and which his music endowed with eternal youth. Since poets are best appreciated by those who travel to the regions that inspired them, as those who have visited the radiant ruins of the Parthenon or the misty splendours of Scotland understand Pindar[10] and Ossian, so Chopin's inspiration can be fathomed only by those who have visited his country. They have seen there the shadow left by passing centuries, witnessing its dusk-like embrace, and met the 'phantom of glory', the frightening and restless spirit that appears in the tales and recollections of past times and haunts his heritage. A similar terror is spread among the peasants of Ukraine by a beautiful virgin that, they say, pale as death, and girdled with crimson, appears daubing with blood the gates of villages doomed to destruction.

Over long centuries, Poland formed a state whose high civilisation was entirely its own and unique of its kind. As different from feudal Germany, its neighbour to the west, as from the conquering Turks that threatened it to the east, Poland was closer to Europe in its chivalric Christianity and eagerness to fight the infidel. By learning lessons in policy, military tactics and weighty discourse from the Byzantines, Poland fused heterogeneous elements from a decaying society with the heroic qualities of Muslim fanaticism, and the sublime virtues of Christian sanctity.[11] The culture of Latin letters together with the taste for Italian and French literature, bestowed upon these strange contrasts the lustre and sheen of classicism. Such a civilisation, even in its final phase, should have its own distinctive style. Little inclined to tales of chivalry and knight-errantry, Poland turned its back on the splendid make-believe of tournaments. Instead, as befitting a nation constantly at war, it reserved brave exploits for its enemies on the battlefield, substituting the games and splendours of the tournament with festivals of a different kind in which magnificent processions were the principal features.

There is certainly nothing new in asserting that national character is revealed in national dances. We believe, however, there are few to compare with the polonaise in its original form for its grand simplicity of outline, in which the energising impulses were conveyed in the episodes that were inserted by individuals into the general framework. As soon as these episodes disappeared, and their vitality was gone, then all that remained was a mechanical and obligatory circuit of the salon with only the skeleton of ancient ceremonial remaining.

We should certainly have hesitated to speak of the polonaise, after the beautiful verses consecrated to it by Mickiewicz and the admirable description he inserted in the last canto of *Pan Tadeusz*, had it not been part of an untranslated work known only to the poet's compatriots.[12] This beautiful epic romance, set at the beginning of this century when there were still many alive who retained the feelings and manners of ancient Poland, unquestionably inspired Chopin many times, its scenes nourishing the emotions he loved to enshrine in his music.

The oldest polonaises, none of which is more than a century old, are so primitive as to have little value as art. Some, bearing no composer's name, are associated with some hero, thus indicating their date, and are mostly solemn and gentle. The polonaise styled '*de*

Kościuszko', is the most widely recognised, and is so closely linked to the memory of its era that we have seen ladies who could not listen to it without weeping.[13] Other polonaises from the same epoch are also so mournful that, on first hearing, they might be taken as the music for a funeral train.

The polonaises of Count Ogiński[14] next appeared and soon acquired great popularity by introducing languor into the mournful vein. Still suffering from sombre colouring, they tempered it with the tenderness of a sad and naive charm. In them, the rhythm subsides and modulation appears as if some procession, once loud, becomes silent and reverential as it passes close to graves where pride and laughter lie stilled. Wandering in these surroundings, love alone survives, repeating the sad refrain that the Bard of Erin snatched from his native air: 'Love born of sorrow, like sorrow is true!'[15] In Ogiński's well known music there may be imagined a similar sentiment, as expressed in two loving sighs, or revealed in eyes moist with tears.

Later, as the polonaise evolved, tombs were left behind as life and vitality returned. Mournful impressions change into memories that return only as echoes, and the imagination no longer evokes spectres that glide carefully lest they awaken the dead. Already in Lipiński's polonaises we hear the heart again beating joyously, dizzily, as it had done before Poland's defeat.[16] His melody is shaped more clearly and exudes the perfume of youth and love in springtime, as it expands into an expressive, dreamy song that whispers only to young hearts of poetic romance. No longer is its purpose to measure the step of dignified and solemn individuals, rather it now appeals to romantic imaginations more given to pleasure than splendour. Mayseder continued along this path and achieved the most sparkling mannerisms and charming liveliness in performance.[17] His imitators, however, have swamped us with pieces entitled 'polonaise' that lack any character to justify the name.

Then, with one stroke, a man of genius, Weber, restored the polonaise's vigorous brilliance and rediscovered all its vanished magnificence.[18] To echo the past in a formula so corrupted, he deployed and united all the resources of his art, not to replicate the music of the past but rather to convey the spirit of the original. He accentuated the rhythm and, dramatising the melody, coloured it with the modulations that it demanded. He energised the polonaise with life, warmth, and passion, while retaining its inherent haughty style, its magisterial dignity and its stylised (yet natural) majesty. His cadences are marked by chords, which sound like the sabres shaken in their scabbards.

The murmur of voices, instead of conveying the lukewarm prattling of love, give way to the deep, full bass tones used to command. Voices such as excite the wild and distant neighing of desert steeds as they impatiently paw the ground, eyes gentle and intelligent yet full of fire, as they so gracefully bear trappings, trimmed with turquoise and rubies, with which Polish lords burden them.[19] Did Weber know historic Poland so well? Had he already visualised a spectacle to make the association? Idle questions! Does not Genius have intuition, and does not poetry always reveal to Genius what lies in its domain?

In approaching his subjects, Weber, with his ardent, highly strung imagination, drew from them, like sap, the essence of their poetry, attaining such mastery that it was difficult to follow him with any hope of achieving the same effects. Chopin, however, surpassed him in inspiration with the number and variety of his works in this genre, and with his more moving style and new harmonic procedures. His polonaises in A major and in A flat major especially resemble Weber's in E major in design and aspect.[20] In others Chopin relinquished this broad style, treating the subject differently and with greater success. Judgement is always a thorny matter. How are the rights of a poet to treat the many facets of his subject to be restrained? In the midst of joy, is he not allowed to be solemn and oppressed, to sing of sorrow having sung of glory, to lament with the bereaved having celebrated with those who rejoice? Surely one aspect of Chopin's superiority was his ability to exploit a theme in all its brilliance and sadness, the phases through which his emotions moved giving him a multiplicity of viewpoints. These shifts, often characterised by frequent suffering, can be followed in a series of polonaises, in which the fertility of his spirit is to be admired even when it is no longer sustained by freshness of inspiration. He did not always limit himself to images presented by imagination and memory. More than once, in contemplating some brilliant throng passing before him, he would become fixated upon some isolated face and, having caught the magic of a glance, delighted in delving into her mysteries and thereafter sing for her alone.

The *Grand Polonaise in F Sharp Minor* must be ranked among Chopin's most vigorous conceptions.[21] In it he inserted a mazurka, an innovation that might have made this wonderful utterance a ballroom success had he not driven frivolity away with a strange fantastic gloom. This work may be read as a tale, in which the first grey glimmerings of a winter dawn give way to the story of a dream after a sleepless night, a dream-poem in which impressions and objects

Chapter 2

succeed each other with strange incoherencies and transitions that recall Byron's poem *A Dream*:

> Dreams in their development have breath,
> And tears, and tortures, and the touch of joy;
> They leave a weight upon our waking thoughts,...
> And look like heralds of Eternity.[22]

The principal theme is a sinister melody, suggestive of the hour that precedes a hurricane as frustrated, defiant exclamations are hurled at the elements. The insistent return of the tonic at the beginning of each bar is reminiscent of volleys of cannon fire in some fierce and distant battle, and thereafter in bar after bar unusual harmonies unfold. Even in the works of the greatest masters we know of no effect as striking as this section, which is suddenly interrupted by a pastoral scene, an idyllic mazurka, full of the scent of lavender and sweet marjoram. Yet far from erasing the memory of the earlier sorrow, the mazurka intensifies, by bitter and ironic contrast, the painful emotions of the listener, to the extent that when the principal theme returns him to the spectacle of the fateful battle, he is freed from the troubling contrast with a naive and inglorious happiness! Like a dream, this improvisation ends with a dismal shudder, leaving the soul with a single dominant impression.

In the *Polonaise-Fantaisie*, belonging to the last period of Chopin's creative life, when his works were overshadowed by a fevered anxiety, there is no hint of bold luminous tableaux.[23] There is no more joyful clatter of cavalry accustomed to victory, of songs that no suppressed thoughts of defeat can silence, of the daring words of would-be victors. An elegiac sadness prevails, broken by alarming movements, melancholy smiles and sudden jerks. There is a restless calm such as is felt by those who have been surprised by an ambush and, surrounded on all sides, cannot see any hope on the vast horizon. Despair mounts in their minds like a copious draft of that Cypriot wine that gives an instinctive rapidity to all gestures, a keener edge to all words, a hotter spark to all emotions, and excites the brain to a pitch of irritability close to delirium. Such tableaux have little merit as art since they, like all depictions of last moments, of death agonies and groans, of muscle contractions when the nerves cease to be the organs of the will, leave man the passive prey of despair! Such images are appalling and the artist should incorporate them into his work only with extreme caution!

CHAPTER 3

CHOPIN'S MAZURKAS, AS FAR as expression is concerned, are notably dissimilar in character to his polonaises. They present another world in which delicate, indefinite and shifting nuances replace rich and vibrant colour, and where purely personal individualised impressions replace the single united impetus of a whole people. The feminine (and effeminate) element is no longer pushed into the background; rather it has a prominence that makes other elements disappear, or at best, serve as its accompaniment. The woman does not appear as a mere follower, but rather as a queen, no longer is she the better part of life, she is all of life. The man, impulsive, proud and arrogant, is drawn to the vortex of pleasure. Yet this pleasure is streaked with melancholy, and the words and music (rarely separated) of national songs reflect the two extremes. Caused by the need to 'gladden misery' (*cieszyc bide*), the two opposites make for a strange and attractive contrast which gives the mazurka the enchantment of a graceful and furtive drama. The words that are sung to these melodies link them more intimately to the life of memory than other dance tunes permit. Fresh and sonorous voices have repeated them many times in many different contexts. Have they not been hummed when travelling, in the woods, on a boat, at emotional moments, or when an encounter, a scene, a hurtful word flashes through the heart – occasions destined to shine in memory, across the most distant years and the darkest regions of the future?

In his mazurkas Chopin seized upon these national melodies with rare pleasure, bringing to them the full benefit of his workmanship and style. Cutting them, like diamonds, into a thousand facets, he exposed all their hidden fire, and then mounted them in glittering settings. What better framework than the mazurka could there have been for him to channel his personal memories into poems, scenes, events and stories which now, thanks to him, make an impact far beyond the land that gave them birth to join those classic forms consecrated by resplendent art?

Chapter 3

To understand how this form suited the shades of feeling that Chopin, with an iridescent hand, brought to it, it is necessary to have seen the mazurka danced in Poland: only thus can one grasp its pride, tenderness and suggestiveness. The man, chosen by his partner, takes hold of her like a prize and, after presenting her for his rivals' admiration, carries her off in a twirling voluptuous embrace that does not conceal the taunting expression of the victor or the blushing vanity of his catch. There are few more delightful spectacles than a ball in Poland when, the mazurka having begun, the attention of the whole room is not distracted by the jostling multitude, but is rather drawn to one couple of equal beauty dashing forward into open space. The gentleman, accentuating his steps as if issuing a challenge, leaves his partner for a moment, the better to contemplate her, only to rejoin her with passionate attentiveness, or to whirl himself round in giddy rapture. Sometimes two couples start at the same time, after which they may change partners; or a third gentleman may turn up clapping his hands to claim one of the ladies from her partner. Then the most brilliant young gentlemen secure the honour of claiming in turn the queens of the ball.

In contrast, the waltz and galop isolate the dancers and offer the spectators only a confused spectacle, while the quadrille is a kind of pass at arms with foils where nonchalant grace is answered with a nonchalant response. The vivacity of the polka, charming as it is, can easily become suggestive; while fandangos, tarantellas and minuets are merely little love-dramas, interesting only to those taking part, in which the gentleman merely displays his lady and the spectators sullenly follow the dancers' affected and meaningless pantomime. In the mazurka, however, everyone is involved and the role of the gentleman yields neither in grace nor in importance to that of his partner.

During the long intervals that separate the successive appearance of the couples, the dancers chat among themselves, so that when their turn comes again they can give their full attention to the spectators. It is to them that the gentleman proudly shows the lady who has favoured him; she too seeks to please them, because their approval is reflected on her partner in the most flattering manner. At the last moment, she seems to transfer their approbation to him by bounding towards him and resting upon his arm, a gesture full of feminine guile and charm and capable of a thousand nuances.

In the mazurka, what varied movements are there in the turns around the ballroom! Beginning at first with a kind of timid hesitation, the lady is poised like a bird about to take to the air. Then sliding for a time on one foot, she skims like a skater on the polished floor before running like a child and taking to the air. Like the divine huntress, with eyes open, head high and swelling bosom, she slices with nimble leaps through the air as a boat cuts the wave, seeming to hang in space.[1] Then she recommences her graceful gliding, while smiling and exchanging a few words with the most favoured spectators, tendering her lovely arms to the partner (who rejoins her) and resumes her agile steps which rapidly carry her from one end of the ballroom to the other. She glides, she runs, she flies. Fatigue colours her cheeks, brightens her glance and slows her step until, breathless and exhausted, she sinks gently into the arms of her partner who, taking her, lifts her momentarily in the air, before they finish the last intoxicating round.

The most varied configurations enliven the triumphal course of the mazurka in which may be seen many an Atalanta as beautiful as any dreamed of by Ovid.[2] In the first chain, all the couples begin by holding hands, then, forming a great circle that briefly whirls around to dazzling effect, they plait a crown in which each lady is a unique flower, while the men's costume, like dark foliage, sets off the diversity of colour. All together, they dash forward animatedly and, in jealous rivalry, haughtily parade before the spectators. After an hour or two, the circle again forms to end the dance, when the participants, often by now infected with a gaiety, like a crackling fire of dried vines, resume the general promenade once more. Despite the accelerated pace, there is not a hint of fatigue among these delicate, tough women whose limbs seem to have the tireless suppleness of steel.

Intuitively, all Polish women possess the magical science of the mazurka. Even the least gifted can improvise it alluringly, since it favours the shy and self-conscious as well as those who know that they are admired and envied. Is this not so because of all the dances it is the most chastely amorous? And the dancers do not ignore the spectators; on the contrary they continually address them. In the mazurka there prevails a mixture of intimate tenderness and mutual vanity, as delicate as it is compelling.

Chopin released the poetic *unknown* [*l'inconnu de poésie*] that was only hinted at in the original themes of the mazurkas. Preserving their rhythm, he ennobled their melody, enlarged their proportions and, with a novel harmonic chiaroscuro, painted in these works, which

Chapter 3

he liked us to call 'pictures from the easel', the many and differing emotions excited by the dance.

Flirtation, vanity, fantasy, fancy, sorrow, passion, awakening feelings, conquest upon which hangs another's fate or favour: all are encountered. Yet how difficult it is to appreciate the infinite degrees of passion, made volatile as much by abandon as by mischief, in the land where the mazurka reigns from the palace to the cottage. In Poland, national characteristics, both virtues and vices, are shared out in such a strange manner that, although essentially the same everywhere, they vary and mingle in such unexpected ways that they become almost unrecognisable! This excessive and capricious diversity among individuals uniquely increases one's curiosity, makes every new contact a challenging study and gives meaning to the slightest incident. Nothing is mediocre, unnoticed or commonplace. Contrasts multiply in natures so restless. Poles have keen and subtle minds, and a sensibility so nourished by adversity that suffering illuminates their hearts like flames in the dark. Chance can bring closer those who were strangers the day before; equally, a momentary aberration or a word can drive apart hearts long united, and give rise to implacable suspicion entertained in secret. As a witty woman once remarked: 'we often play a comedy, to avoid a tragedy!' Constantly, things come to mind that can only be hinted at; generalities are often used to sharpen questions while concealing their true intention; and the most evasive replies are carefully listened to, as with the ringing of metal, and tested for integrity. Pleading for others may be pretence for pleading for self, and flattery may be only disguised demands.

Eventually, constant vigilance becomes a strain, and a tedious flippancy, surprising before its desperate indifference is disclosed, ironically supplements the most spiritual delicacy and the poetic expression of real suffering. This levity eludes quick and easy assessment, being sometimes real, sometimes illusory and, rightly or wrongly, is likened to a veil, whose fabric needs only to be slightly torn to reveal hidden qualities buried in its folds. It follows that eloquence often amounts to no more than serious banter, mere sequins of the mind, a firework display, without any conversational seriousness while, at other times, casual jokes may be sadly serious. Misplaced cheerfulness is closely followed by bitter and intense contemplation, and nothing remains absolutely superficial, although nothing goes without artificial polish either. In Poland, where conversation is an art cultivated to the highest degree and which absorbs much of everyone's time, it is difficult, as one hears a person able to pass in a moment from laughter to grief, to judge the sincerity of what is being said.

Because of these fickle habits of mind, ideas, like moving sandbanks, are rarely to be found at the point at which they were left. This state of affairs lends a special stamp to the most insignificant conversations, as we learned from some Poles who were admired in Parisian society for their resourcefulness in paradox, a skill that most Poles cultivate to some degree. Their inimitable verve constantly changes the garb of truth and fiction, always disguising the one as the other, and lavishes an immense amount of mental effort on trivial occasions. Their troubling panache is akin to the incredible dexterity of Indian jugglers, whose sharp weapons fly glinting through the air and which, with the least error, could become instruments of death. Such skill is full of an anxiety that danger may lurk in the most innocuous circumstance or presumption, and drama may erupt during the most trivial encounters, giving every relationship an unpredictable dimension. Misty uncertainty certainly hovers over the slightest encounters, making them complex, ill defined and over-complicated, and giving them a tension that is straining to be released. These qualities are entangled in the heart of all Poles in an inextricable confusion of patriotism, vanity and love.

And so, what emotions are concentrated in the chance encounters of the mazurka, in which the vaguest desires of the heart are lent excitement, and the most transitory and futile encounters seize the imagination! How could it be otherwise since it is the presence of the women that gives this dance the inimitable sophistication for which, in other countries, they struggle in vain? Are Slav women not truly incomparable? For the most part Polish women are distinguished by a diverse originality; half-Parisian and half-Egyptian, they perhaps possess the secrets of the burning potions of the harem as handed down from mother to daughter. They charm with their Asiatic languor, with the flames of Houri[3] in their eyes and the indolence of a sultana; with their unspoken tenderness and gestures that caress without encouraging; with their slow intoxicating movements and pliant, magnetic poses. They captivate with supple waists and refined etiquette; with touching intonations that summon tears from unknown depths of the heart, and sudden impulses that recall the spontaneity of the gazelle. Moreover, they are intelligent, educated, swift to learn and use all they know; uncannily skilled in reading character, yet they are superstitious and sweet like the beautiful (though ignorant) girls who worship

Chapter 3

the Arabian prophet. Generous and bold, exciting and devout, loving danger and loving love – of which they demand much and give little – they have above all a passion for fame and glory. Heroism delights them and there is perhaps not one among them who would baulk at paying dearly for a glorious deed. And yet, it must be said that many, mysteriously sublime, consign their finest sacrifices and holiest virtues to obscurity. However exemplary their home life as long as their youth lasts, neither private miseries nor secret sorrows suppress the wonderful vivacity of these vulnerable souls. Naturally and socially discreet, they dissimulate with incredible skill, and probe others' souls without revealing their own secrets. The inner contempt they have for those who cannot comprehend them gives them a superiority that enables them to reign artfully over all the hearts they enchant – even to the point of defying and sharing death, exile, prison and the cruellest torture. They are ever faithful, ever tender, and ever devoted.

Polish womanhood is an irresistibly fascinating and honoured composite. As M. de Balzac observed in his celebratory lines: 'she is an angel through love and a devil through fantasy; a child through faith and a sage through experience; a man in intellect and a woman in heart; a giant through hope, a mother through sorrow; and a poet through her dreams'.[4]

Polish women have always inspired fervent homage because they have a poetic understanding of an ideal that sparkles in their conversation. Scornful of the dull and easy satisfaction of merely pleasing, they want the pleasure of admiring those who love them. This need provides romantic nourishment for their desires and makes them hesitate between the world and the cloister where most, at some point in their lives, have seriously considered taking refuge.

There, where such women are sovereign, what feverish words, what hopes and despair, what illusions and intoxication flow in the cadences of the mazurka, each one thrilling in the memory like an echo of a vanished passion or romantic declaration. Who among them has not danced the mazurka with cheeks burning more from emotion than fatigue? What unexpected ties came from long pairings while the music recalled some warrior's name or some historic memory suggested by the words and linked forever to the melody? What vows were exchanged there, what difficult farewells uttered! What brief amours were made and unmade between strangers, who would sadly never meet again, and yet who could not forget each other! What sad affections may have been disclosed in those priceless moments, when beauty is valued higher than wealth, and grace higher than rank! What destinies frustrated by wealth and rank were brought together in encounters that sparkled with the triumph of hidden joys! What conversations, carelessly begun and extended with irony, interrupted by emotion and resumed with innuendo (in which Slav finesse and delicacy excel), have resulted in deep attachments! What confidences have been scattered there in the frankness that strangers share when they are free of the tyranny of convention! And what deceitfully pleasant words, vows, desires and vague hopes were thrown casually to the wind!

As we have pointed out, perhaps it is necessary to understand Chopin's female compatriots to understand the intuitive feelings that suffuse his mazurkas, as well as many of his other compositions. Nearly all of them are filled with the same love vapour that envelops the préludes, nocturnes and impromptus in which they evoke all the stages of passion. The charming lures of coquetry, the imperceptible surrender to inclination, the fickle garlands wrought by fantasy. The fatal despondency of barren joys, born dying recalling black roses, the flowers of mourning that give off a distressing fragrance and which are detached from their fragile stems by the faintest breath. Those pleasures without past or future, snatched from accidental meetings, and the illusions and inexplicable desires that summon us to adventure, like the sharp taste of half ripened fruit that pleases while setting the teeth on edge. They also suggest emotions of infinite range that are reinforced by the true poetic response, innate nobility, beauty, distinction and elegance of those who can feel them.

In most of Chopin's ballades, waltzes and études, as well as in the pieces already mentioned, there is embalmed the memory of an elusive poetry that is so idealised and fragile that it scarcely seems to belong to our world. Rather it seems much closer to the fairy kingdom, as it unveils to us the indiscreet confidences of Peris, Titanias, Ariels, Queen Mabs and all the genii of the air, water and fire, all of whom are, like us, subject to the bitterest setbacks.

At times these works are gay and fantastic like the cavorting of an amorous, teasing sylph, or velvety and shimmering like the skin of a salamander. Some are profoundly disheartening, like souls in torment who can find no prayers for salvation, while others are imbued with despair so inconsolable that we feel ourselves following a Byronic tragedy, as when Jacopo Foscari contemplates his fate in unbearable exile.[5] Then there are those which sound like the spasms

Chapter 3

of suppressed sobs, and yet others which, played only on the black keys, are witty and mocking. The latter recall Chopin's own gaiety who, as a lover of the Attic spirit,[6] dwelt in the upper reaches of mind and spirit, recoiled from vulgar humour, ribaldry and rough play as one might from disgusting creatures repulsive to the eye.

A great variety of subjects and impressions prevail in Chopin's mazurkas. Several are coloured by the sound of jangling spurs, but most of them are distinguishable above all else by the imperceptible rustling of crêpe and gauze under the light breath of the dance, the murmur of fans, and the clinking of gold and diamonds. Some of them seem to depict the fearless yet anxious pleasure of a ball held the day before a battle when, beyond the rhythm of the dance, sighs and faltering, tearful farewells may be heard. Others seem to reveal the anguish, pain and secret torment of those who cannot suppress the clamour of the heart. In still others suppressed terror is heard: fears and presentiments of a love devoured by jealousy that struggles, and survives, to feel its own defeat, disdaining to curse or seek shelter in pity. Elsewhere, there is a whirlwind, a delirium in the midst of which a halting, jerking melody recurs, like the beating of a heart that is swooning, breaking and dying of love. Elsewhere, also, we hear distant fanfares, like distant recollections of glory. And there are some in which the rhythm is as flexible and fluid as the feelings of two young lovers gazing upon a solitary star high in the heavens!

One evening only three of us were together. Chopin had been playing a long time, when one of the most distinguished women in Paris was overcome by solemn contemplation, which she likened to looking at those fields of scattered tombstones in Turkey, whose shade and flowerbeds from afar give the traveller the promise of a smiling garden. She asked Chopin whence came the spontaneous reverence that bowed her heart before these monuments visible only as graceful objects, and by what name did he call the remarkable emotion contained in his compositions, like nameless ashes in splendid urns of finest alabaster? Conquered by the tears that moistened her lovely eyes, Chopin replied, with candour rare for an artist who was so sensitive to all that related to the intimacies buried in the brilliance of his music, that her heart had not deceived her in its melancholy distress. He continued that, whatever his transitory joys, he had never been free from a feeling that had become the seed-bed of his heart, and for which he could find no appropriate expression except in his own language: the Polish word *Żal!* Seeming to relish the sound, he repeated it frequently, as if dwelling on its meaning, its ability to convey the whole gamut of emotions flowing from an intense regret, from repentance to hatred: fruits both blessed and poisoned.

Żal! A strange noun with a strange diversity and an even stranger philosophy! Used in differing contexts, it brings together all the tenderness and humility of a resigned regret as long as it is applied to facts and objects. Once it is applied to man, it can signify seething malice, censure, thoughts of vengeance and an implacable menace that feeds on sterile bitterness!

In truth, *żal* continually tinges Chopin's oeuvre with a sheen sometimes cool and sometimes glowing. It is never far from even his sweetest reveries, those in which Berlioz, that Shakespearian genius who understands all extremes, glimpsed 'divine endearments' [*divines chatteries*]. Such endearments belong to semi-oriental women, with which men are cradled by their mothers; cuddled by their sisters; enchanted by their mistresses, all of which later makes the advances of other women appear insipid or coarse, and gives rise to the justifiable boast: '*Niema iak Polki!*' ('Polish women are unequalled'!).[7] 'Divine endearments', at once generous and grudging, in which lie the secret of what makes these beings adorable, impress upon the enamoured heart the rocking and uncertain motion of a boat with neither rigging nor oars.

Chopin, in performance, beautifully conveyed this pulsation, giving the melody an undulating effect, like a skiff on the crest of a powerful wave. Early in his writings, he described this style, which gave such an individual stamp to his playing, with the term *tempo rubato*, being a tempo stolen or interrupted, abrupt and languid, flickering as a breathed-upon flame. In his later publications he stopped using this marking, persuaded that an intelligent performer would grasp this rule of irregularity. Thus all his compositions should be played with this accentuated and measured swaying, the secret of which is difficult to grasp for those who did not hear him play. He seemed eager to impart this *rubato* playing style to his many pupils, particularly perhaps to his compatriots. Among them, it was the women rather than the men who grasped it with that competence that they have for everything relating to feeling and poetry and an intuitive understanding of his thought that allowed them to follow all the fluctuations within his pure blue space.

CHAPTER 4

We have written already of Chopin's works, in which his genius, vibrant with immortal feelings, sometimes vainly struggled with grief. We have also discussed those works into which he poured, like tears into a lachrymatory,[1] all the memories of his youth, the inclinations of his heart, the ardour of his hopes and all his unspoken desires. We have spoken too of those works that take us into the world of Dryads, Oreads and Oceanides[2] where our dulled perceptions and blunted sensitivity cannot follow. We now ought to turn to his talent in performance, if only we had the sad courage to exhume those emotions (interlaced with the most intimate memories) and paint their shrouds with the colours they deserve. We feel it pointless, for what would we achieve? How can we convey, to those who never heard him, his ineffable poetry, as subtle and penetrating as the delicate and exotic Ethiopian calla or verbena – fragrances that can be appreciated only in intimate settings away from the stifling throng?

Chopin knew that his talent, in style, imagination and purity of expression recalled Nodier, as in *La Fée au miettes* and *Les Lutins d'Argail*,[3] in which seraphines and dianes whisper secret grievances and ill-defined dreams. He knew that he did not move the multitude or make an impact on the masses. (For they are like a sea of fiery lead which, malleable only by fire, requires a sturdy labourer's arm to be poured into moulds, where the metal assumes a new form of thought and feeling). He knew that he was truly appreciated only in those all-too-rare gatherings in which all his hearers were prepared to follow him into those spheres where all is charming magic, mad surprise and dreams come true: that place where he sought refuge with such delight. He once confided to a friend, an artist who has since performed a great deal, 'I am not suited to give concerts, the public intimidates me, I feel suffocated by its breath, paralysed by looks, and am mute before those anonymous faces. But you, you are destined for it, because when you do not win over the public, you are able to overwhelm it'.

Liszt's *Chopin*

Aware of the constraints imposed upon him by the nature of his talent, Chopin rarely played in public and, except for his *début* concerts at the beginning of 1831 in Vienna and Munich, thereafter performed only in Paris. He was unable to travel because of his health, which was so weak that he appeared to be dying for months at a time. During his only journey to the south, taken in the hope that the climate would do him good, his condition was frequently so alarming that several innkeepers, believing his consumption to be highly contagious, demanded advance payment for bedding so that it could be later burned.

We believe that Chopin's concerts exhausted his physical constitution less than they did his artistic sensibilities, and that his voluntary sacrifice of resounding success concealed an inner pain. Although he had a very clear sense of his own great superiority, the audience's response did not give him the quiet certainty that he was fully appreciated. Popular acclaim was never his, and he must have asked himself to what extent the distinguished salons of the elite compensated, in the enthusiasm of their applause, for the great public that he chose to avoid. Few understood him, but did the few understand him enough? A discontent of which he himself did not understand the source secretly undermined him, and we have seen him almost shocked by glowing tributes. All that he was entitled to claim never came to him in great outpourings and he was sometimes vexed by isolated compliments. Indeed, he often brushed them off, like annoying specks of dust, with polite phrases, making it clear that he felt not only little applauded but badly applauded, and that he preferred to be undisturbed in the solitude of his feelings.

Because Chopin was too subtle a connoisseur of mockery, too clever in derision to expose himself to sarcasm, he never assumed the mantle of misunderstood genius. He concealed the wounds to his pride with such outward grace and satisfaction that their existence was scarcely suspected. We assume that the increasing rarity of his concerts was due more to a wish to avoid occasions that failed to bring the tributes he deserved, rather than to any physical frailty – which was severely tested both by his constant teaching and by the many hours he spent at his piano.

Unfortunately, the unquestionable advantages to an artist that comes from cultivating a select audience are lessened by the meagreness of its approbation. The chill that enfolds the favour of the elite, like fruit topping a dessert, and the unruffled calm of its warmest

Chapter 4

enthusiasm, was never enough for him. The poet, torn from his lonely inspiration, can regain it only in the lively, attentive, and more responsive interest of his audience. He can never hope to reach for it in the cold glances of an areopagus assembled to judge him.[4] His task is to move his listeners, so that his emotions find an instinctive response in them as he draws them on in his flight towards the infinite – as the leader of a flock of birds, giving the signal to depart, is followed by the rest towards more lovely shores.

Had it been otherwise. Had Chopin everywhere received the homage and admiration he deserved; had he, like so many other pianists, been heard by international audiences; had he won loud ovations that create shrines wherever people celebrate merit, honour and genius; and had thousands instead of mere hundreds acclaimed him: then we would not now need to detail his success.

What are mere bouquets to those whose brows demand the laurel of immortality? Ephemeral sympathies and passing praises are hardly to be mentioned beside a memorial that claims the highest glory. Chopin's creations are destined to go far in distance and time, bringing the joys, comforts and warm emotions of artworks to the suffering, damaged, faltering, persevering and believing souls to whom they are dedicated. Thus they establish a continuous bond among higher natures in whatever place or time they live, those spirits who are misconstrued when they remain silent and often misunderstood when they speak!

'There are different garlands', wrote Goethe, 'even some that may be picked while taking a walk.' Yet such garlands only charm momentarily with their fragrant freshness. They are insufficient acknowledgement for what Chopin achieved through unremitting, exemplary effort, through a profound love of art, and through the sad emotions that he expressed so well.

Chopin never pettily sought those garlands of which more than one of us boasts. He was a pure, generous and compassionate man filled with a single sentiment, the noblest one on earth: the love of country. Since he moved among us, like a ghost devoted to all that Poland possessed in poetry, let us pay reverence at his tomb. Let us not throw upon it artificial flowers! Let us not cast upon it paltry, easily won garlands! Let us lift our hearts before his coffin! Let us learn from him to reject all but the highest ambitions, to concentrate our efforts on making a deeper mark than the fashion of the day! Let us renounce, for ourselves, in the sad times in which we live, all that is unworthy in art, all that will not endure, all that does not possess the eternal and immaterial beauty essential for art to make itself resplendent. Let us remember the prayer of the ancient Dorians, a petition so simple, pious and poetic, with which they asked their gods *to give them the Good through Beauty*.[5] Instead of striving to please audiences at all costs, let us rather exert ourselves, like Chopin, to leave a divine echo of what we have felt, loved and suffered! And finally, let us learn from his memory to demand of ourselves what will give us respect in the mystical city of art rather than to seek in the present, without regard for the future, those meaningless garlands that are scarcely amassed before they are withered and forgotten!

Instead of these, the fairest tributes that an artist could receive in his lifetime were placed into Chopin's hands by illustrious equals to express the admiration of a public still more limited than the musical aristocracy that frequented his concerts. The famous names within this group bowed before him like the kings of various empires gathered to honour one of their own, rendering him the full homage that was his due. It could not have been otherwise in France where hospitality discerns, with such unerring taste, the true status of its guests.

The most distinguished minds in Paris frequently met in Chopin's salon. Such gatherings that were distinctly not of the mind-numbing variety, such as idle, stiff and bored circles arrange, in which gaiety, sparkle, and enthusiasm come to no one, and certainly not to genuine artists. Yet the latter too, who are infected by a sacred malady, a numbing paralysis and pain, occasionally need their own firework displays of Roman candles, Bengal lights, cascades of fire or make-believe dragons! Sadly, poets and artists, like everyone else, find cheerfulness and sparkle hard to find! Yet a few, the most fortunate among them, it is true, are more privileged. They have the happy gift of mastering their inner pain and bear their burden lightly, being able to laugh with their fellow travellers about the difficulties of the journey, or to maintain a kindly serenity which, like a tacit pledge of hope and consolation, revives and encourages. While they remain in this tranquil state, they have a freedom of spirit that can become more intense since it contrasts strongly with their usual tedium and care-worn distraction.

Chopin belonged to neither of these categories. As a host, he deployed the innate grace of Polish welcome, which not only observed the usual codes of hospitality but also went further by putting every personal consideration aside to attend to his guests' enjoyment. It was delightful to visit him because he was always charming and, knowing

Chapter 4

how to put his visitors at ease, he placed everything he possessed at their disposal. His was an unlimited generosity, such as even a simple Slav ploughman offers in his hovel and who compensates for a lack of splendour with a familiar phrase (also repeated before even the most sumptuous banquets of the nobility): '*czym bohat, tym*'. Translated, this adage means: 'deign to pardon all that is unworthy of you, but I place all my humble riches at your feet'.[6] It is a saying still uttered with a native dignity by those who preserve the meticulous and picturesque aspects of the ancient manners of Poland.

Once acquainted with Polish hospitality, our meetings at Chopin's salon may be better imagined, with their expansiveness, informality and good cheer that left no flat or bitter aftertaste, no ill humour behind. Though he avoided society, he displayed a charming consideration when guests entered his home, where, without appearing to focus on any one individual, he succeeded in demonstrating his courtesy and devoted attentiveness to all.

There is no question that Chopin had a certain misanthropic reluctance to opening his door and his piano, even when asked by the most loyal and respectful friends. Accordingly, many of us still remember our first impromptu evening with him, despite his refusal, when he was living in the Chaussée d'Antin. His salon, when thus unexpectedly invaded, was lit by a few candles gathered around a Pleyel piano, an instrument that he particularly favoured for its slightly veiled (yet silvery) sonority and its easy touch, and which sounded somewhat like those glass harmonicas built by the craftsmen of Germany.

The corners of the room were left in darkness so that the room extended into a shadowy space. In the dim light, a piece of furniture draped with a white cover could be glimpsed standing like a spectre come to listen to the sounds that had summoned it. The light concentrated around the piano fell on the floor rippling, like a spreading wave, until it mingled with the flickering firelight, from which burly orange flames occasionally erupted, like curious gnomes drawn there by their own special language. A single portrait, that of a pianist (an admiring and sympathetic friend), seemed a constant listener to the ebb and flow of the music, which moaned and roared, murmured and died upon the instrument near which it hung. The reflecting surface of the mirror, by ethereal chance, duplicated the image for us, reflecting a handsome oval face with silky curls that has been much copied and even engraved.

Gathered around the piano in a lit area were several figures of great renown. Heine, the saddest of humorists, listened with the interest of a compatriot to the tales that Chopin told him, of that mysterious land that also haunted his ethereal imagination and which he too had explored. Chopin and Heine understood each other intuitively, so that to any murmured question the musician replied with surprising passages on the keyboard. First, the poet seemed to ask of news of the laughing nymph: 'Does she continue to drape her silvery veil around her green hair with such annoying coquetry.' Then he asked: 'Does the marine god still pursue this cheerful naiad with his ridiculous love?'[7] Well-informed about the enchantments to be seen *over there – over there*, he asked: 'Do the roses still burn there with a constant flame?' and 'Do the trees still sing in the moonlight?' After Chopin had answered, they both, having spoken much of that aerial homeland, remained silent and sad, seized with homesickness. When Heine fell into this mood, he likened himself to that Dutch captain of the ghost ship forever consigned to sail the cold seas with his crew.[8] The Dutchman who: 'sighing in vain for the spices, the tulips, the hyacinths, the pipes of Holland. *Amsterdam! Amsterdam! When shall we again see Amsterdam?* they cry on board, while the tempest, howling in the rigging, tosses them about forever on their watery hell'. 'I understand', added Heine, 'the unfortunate captain's rage when he once exclaimed: *Oh! if ever I should return to Amsterdam! I would rather become a bollard on one of its streets than be forced to leave again!* Poor van Decken!'

Heine well knew all that poor van der Decken had suffered on his terrible, eternal voyage upon an ocean that held his ship as if by an invisible anchor from which he could never break free. When so inclined he would tell us of the sorrows and hopes, despair and agonies of the unfortunates on board this unhappy vessel, because he too had walked its decks, led on by some enamoured *undine*.[9] And when, as a guest in her undersea forest of coral and palace of pearl, he became morose, bitter and caustic, to brighten his moods she would offer him some spectacle worthy of a lover who dreamt of more wonders than her whole kingdom contained.

Heine had travelled the world on this indestructible ship. He had crossed the poles where the aurora borealis, the brilliant visitor of long nights, brushes its broad scarf over immense stalactites of eternal ice. He had visited the tropics where, during the short nights, the Zodiacal triangle[10] replaces with its mystical light the scorching

Chapter 4

rays of the oppressive sun. He had sailed those latitudes where life is harsh and where it is devoured, becoming familiar with the celestial wonders that mark the course of those sailors who make for no port. Lodged in the rudderless stern, he had scanned the heavens from the two Bears (majestically overhanging the north) to the brilliant Southern Cross beyond which is the Antarctic desert extending above and below, leaving the desperate eye with nothing to see but an empty sky above a shoreless sea. He had long followed in the blue void the fleeting trails of shooting stars, like fireflies on high, and comets on their countless lonely orbits that are feared for their strange splendour. He had followed too that distant star, Aldebaran[11] – which, like the sinister glint in the eye of an enemy, seems to glare upon our globe without daring to approach it – as well as other, more radiant planets that warm and comfort with their light.

Heine had seen all these things and much else besides of which he would talk. He was present at the wild cavalcade of Herodias,[12] he had been to the court of the King of the Elves and to the Garden of the Hesperides as well as to those places inaccessible to mortals.

Seated next to Heine that evening was Meyerbeer,[13] a composer who has long since exhausted all compliments. A creator of cyclopean harmonies, he still savoured the detailed arabesques that enveloped Chopin's thoughts.

Further away sat Adolphe Nourrit,[14] that noble artist who was both ascetic and passionate, a devout and almost austere Catholic, he dreamt of the future with a medieval fervour, so that in his last years he denied his talent to all superficial music. He served art with a chaste and fervent respect, embracing it in all its many guises as a holy tabernacle *the beauty of which flows from the splendour of truth*. Already creased by a melancholy passion for the beautiful, Nourrit's brow was also mottled with the shadow of mortality, by the onset of the despair that always comes too late for human remedy. Man: so curious of the heart's secrets yet so inept at divining them.

Hiller, one of Chopin's truest friends, was also there.[15] It should be remembered that his talent was akin to Chopin's since, before he published his large-scale works (among them the remarkable oratorio *The Destruction of Jerusalem*), he wrote works mostly for the piano. Some of them, entitled *Études,* are vigorous sketches of the most polished kind and recall those studies of foliage in which landscape painters create short poems of light and shade in a single tree, a single branch or a single line, all happily and boldly handled.

Eugène Delacroix remained silent and absorbed with the apparitions that filled the air. Was he pondering what palette, what brushes, what canvas he must use, to give them life in his art? Was he asking himself whether he needed a canvas woven by Arachne,[16] a brush made from the eyelashes of a fairy, or a palette covered with the tints of rainbow mist, to make such a sketch possible? Did he then inwardly smile at his imaginings, while yielding to the impressions from which they sprung, through the attraction that some great talents feel for genius that contrasts with their own?

Then there was the elderly Niemcevicz, a revered survivor of times past who appeared nearest to the grave among us, who listened intently to the *Historical Songs* [*Chants historiques*] that Chopin had written for him.[17] Under Chopin's fingers the popular themes of the Polish bard were heard anew: the shock of arms, the song of victors, the hymns of celebration, the lament of illustrious prisoners and the ballads for dead heroes – all recalling the long and glorious history of the Polish nation. And the old man, taking illusion for the present, believed that the past had come to life again. Finally, dark and silent, and apart from all others, could be glimpsed the motionless silhouette of Mickiewicz, that Dante of the North who always seemed to find 'the salt of the stranger bitter and his stairs hard to climb'.[18]

Sunk in an armchair, resting her elbows on a console, was Madame Sand, curiously attentive and subdued. She listened with all the intensity of her fiery genius, endowed with that faculty given only to a chosen few, of recognising the beautiful in whatever form of nature or art it might take. This second sight is widely acknowledged as a higher gift in inspired women. It strips off the externals of form so that the invisible essence, the incarnate soul – the ideal that the poet or artist conjures up in the torrent of notes, layers of colour, the chiselling of stone or the rhythms of verse – may be contemplated. This ability, in its supreme manifestations, is a rare oracle that is aware of the past while looking into the future. It is a power that exempts those special individuals from the baggage of technical science that most people have to drag toward the mystical regions which they can reach in a single bound, a gift that springs less from the mysteries of science than from frequent communing with nature.

In these encounters with Creation lie the attraction and nobility of rural life. There, the revelations concealed in the infinite harmonies of shapes and sounds, of light, of tumult and twitter, of terror and voluptuousness, of a profusion of contrasts which, when faced with

Chapter 4

a fearless courage might hold a key to the relationship between our senses and feelings. To have listened from an early age, as did Mme Sand, to the murmuring with which Nature initiates the chosen into its mystic rites, is one of the essential attributes of the poet. But to learn from Nature what may be drawn from it in their creative work requires a still more subtle gift, and she, as woman and a poet, possessed it by a double right: through the intuition of her heart, and her genius.

Mme Sand, whose energetic personality and dazzling genius inspired in the frail Chopin an admiration that consumed him, is the only name that we wish to summon from the limbo of the past – that place of vague images and sympathies, of uncertain projects and beliefs, and of some stillborn feeling! Alas! Among the interests, trends and desires that filled an epoch in which so many refined souls and brilliant intellects were fortuitously gathered together, how many had enough vitality to resist and defeat the mortality that surrounds every idea and feeling? Of the many feelings that made noble hearts beat faster, how many were exposed to the annihilating curse: 'Happy, oh, happy were it dead! Far happier had it never been born'? There are perhaps no feelings or ideas if fetched from their graves, like the suicide lover in Mickiewicz's poem who returns from the dead only to renew his earthly sufferings, that could live again without scars and bruises disfiguring its primal beauty and soiling its innocence.[19] Among these gloomy ghosts how many would still have enough beauty and candour, enough enchantment and radiance, not to be disowned by those that had given them life and experienced their joys and torments? What a sepulchral roll-call would be necessary to discover which had produced good and ill in those hearts which gave them liberal sanctuary, and which they beautified and shattered, cheered and devastated, according to their whims.

If among Chopin's guests, all of whom bore the heavy responsibility of fame, there was but one who bequeathed to art only what was rapt and divine in his inspiration, then let us celebrate his work, especially valuable with popular appeal, as affirming our faith in the creative spirit. Did not the great Italian poet describe genius as 'a stronger impress of divinity'?[20] Let us therefore bow before all who have been thus deeply stamped with the divine seal, but let us especially revere with the most intimate affection those who, like Chopin, exercised their supremacy solely to give life and expression to the most beautiful feelings.

CHAPTER 5

A NATURAL CURIOSITY ATTACHES itself to the biographies of those who glorify noble feelings in artworks, efforts that transform them into symbols of nobility and greatness that shine like brilliant meteors in the eyes of the delighted masses. In the public mind, such figures become symbols of nobility and greatness, who know no other sentiments, and a need is created to see those ideals at work in their lives. When artworks reveal that the poet seems exquisitely to feel all that inspires him, intuiting all that is concealed by human nature – when he paints love as youth dreams it and regret as the old despair of it – when his genius calmly rises above events, finding the threads by which the most complicated knots can be untied – when he soars above both greatness and disaster towards summits that others cannot reach – when it is apparent that he possesses the secret of the most subtle tenderness and the noblest courage – then this question arises: does his insight spring from the deepest feelings or from clever intellectual abstraction and mind-games?

Other questions then follow. How do the lives of those men who love beauty differ from those of ordinary people? How does poetic splendour struggle with the realities and material interests of life? How are the emotions of ineffable love kept free from poisonous bitterness, and how are they protected from frivolity and fickleness that result in neglect? Are they who feel noble indignation always just? Do they who glorify integrity never sell their consciences? Are they who sing of honour never timid? And are they who admire fortitude never compromised by their own weakness?

There are many eager to know how far those who are entrusted with maintaining our faith in the great and noble feelings enshrined in art strike a balance between honour, loyalty and delicacy and the advantages secured at their expense. Thus when some misfortune gives support to the words of such critics, with what haste are the poet's loveliest ideas declared vain deceits! How they flaunt their wisdom in preaching doctrines, both premeditated and hypocritical,

Chapter 5

of a perpetual and hidden contradiction between words and deeds! With what cruel joy do they cite such instances to those weak and disturbed souls whose youthful hopes (or flagging will and fading convictions) still try to escape these sad conclusions! What disappointment such souls experience when faced with such seductive insinuations, when they are led to believe that hearts most devoted to the sublime, most initiated in delicate susceptibilities, most affected by the beauty of innocence, have nevertheless by their actions denied the sincerity of their songs! With what agonising doubts are they filled by such contradictions! What mockery is poured on their misery by those who repeat *poetry is what might have been*! For Poetry is no mere shadow of our imagination magnified and projected on the elusive outline of the impossible! 'Poetry and Truth' (*Dichtung und Wahrheit*)[1] are not incompatible elements, destined to move in parallel and never meet; as Goethe said of a contemporary poet, 'having lived to create poems, he had made his life a poem' (*Er lebte Dichtend und Dichtete lebend*). Goethe was himself too true a poet not to know that poetry exists only because its eternal reality is found in the finest instincts of the human heart.

Like nobility, genius has responsibilities (*génie oblige*), as we once had occasion to say.[2] Although the cold austerity and disinterestedness of certain artistic figures can win the admiration of reflective natures, where will more passionate and quixotic individuals, those temperaments who seek the joys of honour or pleasure regardless of price, find their models? They reject the authority of their elders, accusing them of monopolising the world to satisfy their own withered passions, of pronouncing upon causes that they do not understand, and of promulgating rules in spheres that they cannot enter! Instead they turn to others for answers. They question those who have drunk from the spring of grief that gushes from beneath the slopes where the soul has built itself an eyrie. They pay no heed to the sombre silences of those who practise the good without exalting the beautiful. Does passionate youth not have the leisure to interpret silences and to resolve its problems? The throbbing of the youthful heart is too rapid to give an insight into the hidden sufferings, the secret and lonely struggles that may be detected even in the quiet glance of a good man. Restless souls cannot understand the calm simplicity of the just, or the heroic smile of the stoic: to them enthusiasm and emotion are essential. For those who prefer the finality of action to the tedium of argument, only images can persuade, metaphors carry conviction and tears convince.

They turn with avid curiosity only to those artists and poets who move them with images, sweep them up with metaphors and inflame them with enthusiasms. It is from them that they demand the ultimate thrill.

Yet excessive excitement can be dangerous. Who among those who have sensed its destructive power has not sought to ascertain what was merely diverting or speculative, and find reassurance that their aspirations were still alive and sincere and that their emotional world was still intact? At such times denigration is not idle; it seizes greedily upon faults, frailties and neglect, and overlooks nothing. It grasps its prey, probes shortcomings and scorns inspiration, granting it no rights except that of providing entertainment, and denying it the power to guide our actions and determine our assent or refusal. Denigration, mocking and cynical, knows how to winnow history! Discarding the good grain, it carefully gathers the bad in order to scatter its black seed over brilliant pages where are to be found the heart's purest desires and the imagination's noblest dreams. Then it demands with victorious irony: 'what is this pure wheat that germinates so poorly?' 'What are these empty words that engender only sterile feelings?' 'What purpose has these excursions to a realm where no fruit is picked?' 'What is the value of emotion and enthusiasm which culminate in self-interest and egotism?'

With what arrogant derision does denigration draw together and examine the poet's noble impulse and his unworthy humiliation, his beautiful song and his guilty superficiality! What superiority it assumes over the hard-won success of worthy people (whom it likens to crustacea, a lower life form), as well as over the pomposity of those who pursue material wellbeing, the pursuit of material comforts, the contentment of vanity and impulsive pleasures! How skilfully does denigration triumph over the hesitations, the doubts and the aversions of those who still believe it possible to unite vivid feelings, passionate impressions, intellectual gifts and poetic meaning with integrity of character and an unblemished life that would never undermine the poetic ideal!

How then not to be moved by the noblest sadness whenever a poet is disobedient to the inspiration of the Muses, those guardian angels of talent, who would gladly teach him to make his own life his finest poem? What disastrous scepticism, regrettable dejection and grievous apostasy follow the faltering of genius! Yet the voice of denigration deliberately confuses these lapses with grovelling servility and

Chapter 5

shameless boastfulness! What a sacrilege! For if the poet's actions have sometimes belied his song has not his song occasionally denied his actions? May not his work contain qualities that far outweigh obnoxious behaviour? Evil is contagious, but good is fertile! The poet, despite compromising his convictions with unworthy indulgence, still glorifies feelings in his works that give them an influence more far-reaching than his private life. Have not these works consoled and edified more souls than the vicissitudes of his private life have demoralised? Art is more powerful than the artist. His creations have a life independent of his shaky will, for they are manifestations of immutable beauty and, more durable than he, pass from generation to generation, intact and incorruptible, containing the potential for the artist's redemption.

If alas, there be many among them who have immortalised their sensibility and aspirations through commanding eloquence while stifling their hopes and abusing their talent – have not they too encouraged others to pursue a noble course through their works of genius! Indulgence alone would perhaps be enough justice for them, but how hard it is to call for justice! How disagreeable it is to have to defend what should be admired, and to excuse what should be venerated!

With what sweet pride does a friend and artist recall the career of one who was free of wounding conflicts, contradictions, errors and extremes. One who worked with ease within firm strictures, honoured and honourable laws, while maintaining an elevation of the soul that acknowledged no reverse or self-betrayal! In this respect Chopin's memory will be doubly cherished by the friends and fellow-artists who knew him, by those unknown friends won over by his music, and by those artists who, coming after, shall win glory in being worthy of him!

Chopin's personality, in all its complexity, did not conceal a single impulse that was not dictated by the most delicate sense of honour and the noblest understanding of the affections. Yet there was never a nature more given to eccentricities, whims and moody peculiarities. His imagination was passionate, his feelings tended towards violence and his constitution was weak and sickly. Who can gauge the suffering caused by such contrasts? It must have been impossible to bear but he never showed it! He kept his secret, hiding it from all under the inscrutable calm of proud resignation.

Chopin's constitutional frailty imposed upon him the feminine martyrdom of suffering in silence, and freighted his destiny with certain other feminine traits. Excluded by his health from the breathless bustle of everyday living, he built himself a refuge away from the noisy mainstream. No adventures or complications disfigured a life that was kept simple against formidable odds. Feelings and impressions were far more important to him than the shifts and setbacks of daily existence. The lessons that he gave, regularly and assiduously, amounted to a domestic routine that he conscientiously followed. He poured out his soul in composition as others do in prayer: expressing in music those effusions of the heart, that unexpressed sorrow, that indescribable grief, which pious souls pour into their communion with God. He expressed in his works what others only say on their knees: those mysteries of passion and pain that man understands without words because they cannot be expressed in words.

The care that Chopin took to avoid the inconsequential and chaotic zigzags of existence deprived his life of incident. A few blurred lines wreathe his image as if in a bluish haze, disappearing under the finger that would touch or trace its outline. He involved himself in no initiative, drama or complication. He exercised no decisive influence upon the life of another. His will never encroached upon any desire, nor did his mind fetter or control that of another. He neither tyrannised over another's heart nor placed a conquering hand upon another's destiny. He sought nothing and scorned to ask for anything. Like Tasso, he might say *'brama assai, poco spera, e nulla chiede'* [loved much, hoped little, and desired nought].[3] He avoided ties and friendships that might have dragged or pushed him into more turbulent spheres. Ready to give all, he never gave himself. Perhaps he knew what exclusive devotion, what unlimited affection he might have deservedly inspired and shared! Perhaps he thought, like other aspiring souls, that, if love and friendship are not all, then they are nothing! Perhaps it cost him more effort to accept and share these feelings than to remain ever faithful to his hopeless ideal! If this was so, no one ever knew, because he hardly ever spoke of love or friendship. He was not exacting. Even his most intimate acquaintances never managed to enter that retreat where his soul, away from everyday life, dwelt in a refuge so hidden that its existence was hardly suspected.

In his everyday relations and conversation he seemed interested only in what concerned others, refraining from imposing his personality on theirs. Although he devoted little time to others, what he did spare was devoted entirely. No one ever asked him of his dreams, hopes or desires since, in his presence, no one had the opportunity

Chapter 5

or temerity to raise such topics! Rarely did he converse on emotional subjects, rather he glided over them and, since he was ungenerous with his time, his conversation was easily taken up with the detail of daily life. He was careful, moreover, never to allow himself to slip into digressions of which he himself might become the subject. His personality rarely excited curiosity, probing thoughts, or keen scrutiny since his way was too pleasing to incur such reflection. His appearance and bearing were harmonious and require no special comment. His blue eyes were more spiritual than dreamy and his sweet fine smile never tended to bitterness. The transparent delicacy of his complexion captivated the eye, his fair hair was soft and silky, his nose was curved, his bearing was distinguished, and his manners had such an aristocratic stamp that he was instinctively treated like a prince. His gestures were many and graceful, his voice always subdued, his stature was small, and his limbs were weak. His appearance recalled the convolvulus with its slight stem and divinely coloured cups, whose petals are so fragile that they are torn by the slightest contact.

In society, he displayed an evenness of mood typical of those who are untroubled by the need to press an interest. He was usually gay and his caustic spirit was capable of probing, quickly and deeply, into the ridiculous. In mimicry he was inexhaustibly droll and often amused others by parodying the musical mannerisms and idiosyncrasies of certain virtuosi, imitating their gestures, movements and facial expressions with a talent that instantly conveyed their personalities. On such occasions his own features would become unrecognisable as they underwent the strangest transformations – although when imitating the ugly and grotesque he never lost his own innate gracefulness. Grimacing was never taken so far as to disfigure him, and his gaiety was so much more piquant because he always kept within the limits of perfect good taste. Even in moments of complete familiarity, unseemly language or an ill-judged quip could shock him.

By totally avoiding conversation of which he was the subject, and by a constant discretion with regard to his own feelings, Chopin left an impression of one who charmed without fear of obligation – or concern that a flourish of mirth would be followed by melancholy confidences, as with those beings of whom it may be said: *ubi mel, ibi fel* [where there is honey, there is gall].[4] His presence was always welcomed, since he thus so busied himself with externals that his inner personality remained apart, insular and unapproachable under a smooth and polished surface that was impossible to probe.

There were, however, rare moments when we caught him so deeply moved that his complexion became pale and almost cadaverous. Yet even when seized by the strongest emotions he retained his self-control, and was reluctant to discuss what had affected him. A minute of recovery was always enough for him to conceal his first reaction. The actions that followed thereafter, whatever the spontaneous grace that he imparted to them, were always the result of a reflection and a will that mastered the bizarre conflict between moral energy and physical weakness within him. The constant control exercised over the violence of his character recalled the sad superiority of those who look for inner strength in self-restraint and isolation, knowing the pointlessness of angry outbursts and too protective of their passions to reveal them gratuitously.

Chopin knew how to forgive in the noblest manner and no rancour remained in his heart for those who had hurt him. But since such wounds struck deeply into his soul they painfully festered there so that, long after he had forgotten their cause, he still felt their secret bite. Nevertheless, by subjecting his feelings to what he thought *ought to be* rather than to what *really is* he could outwardly seem grateful for services offered in friendship, better intentioned than informed, that often went against his sensitivities. The faults of innocent awkwardness are, however, the hardest for nervous temperaments to bear, condemned, as they are, to repress their anger without ever knowing its true causes. Since to deviate from what appeared to him to be the most honourable course of conduct was a temptation that he never had to resist, when confronted with more energetic and decisive personalities than his own he concealed the stress that stemmed from contact with them.

His reserve in conversation extended to all controversial subjects. His patriotism was revealed in the direction taken by his talent, in his friendships, in his choice of favourite pupils and in the frequent and significant services that he enjoyed giving to his compatriots. We cannot recall that he took any pleasure in expressing his patriotic feelings. If he sometimes spoke about political ideas, which in France are so frequently discussed, and so fiercely attacked and so passionately defended, it was to point out what he thought was wrong in the opinions of others rather than to offer his own views. In constant touch with some of the most important politicians of the day, he confined his relations with them to one of personal warmth completely free from conformity of opinion.

Chapter 5

In Chopin's eyes, democracy represented a collection of elements too heterogeneous, too worrying in its savage power, to win his sympathies. When, more than twenty years ago, the eruption of social questions was compared to a new barbarian invasion, he was peculiarly and painfully struck by this terrible comparison.[5] He despaired of obtaining Rome's safety from these modern Attilas, of preserving from destruction its art and monuments – civilisation, in a word, that elegant refined and indolent life of which Horace sang.[6] He followed events at a distance with an unexpected perspicacity that often enabled him to predict what those better informed had little anticipated. Yet, when such insights slipped out, he never expanded on them, his brief comments attracting little attention until they were justified by events. His shrewd good sense had convinced him of the emptiness of most political speeches, theological discussions and philosophical digressions. Thus he practised the favourite maxim of a distinguished man, the Marquis Jules de Noailles, whose remark from the wisdom of misanthropic old age once startled our youthful inexperience but which has struck us since with its sad truth: 'that it is scarcely possible to talk about anything to anybody'.[7]

Sincerely religious and attached to Catholicism, Chopin never approached this subject, holding his beliefs without parading them. One could know him for a long time without having any idea what his religious opinions were. *Il mondo va da se* [the world goes its own way] he seemed to tell himself. We have watched him for long periods in the midst of noisy and animated discussions from which he silently abstained. In the passion of debate he was forgotten, while we, for our part, often left the argument to fix our attention on his face, which imperceptibly contracted when subjects important to our very existence were discussed with such energy that it seemed that our fates were then being decided upon. At such times, he appeared like a passenger on board of a storm-tossed ship, watching the horizon and the stars, thinking of his distant country, following the actions of the crew and counting their mistakes, yet without the strength to help save the vessel.

Only in the name of art did Chopin drop his reserve and break his studied silence and customary neutrality. On this issue alone would he not flinch from voicing his opinions and exerting his influence. And when he did so, he tacitly gave proof that he considered himself as having the legitimate authority of a great artist on matters arising from his talent and vocation, and left no doubt as to how he viewed them. For some years he injected his arguments with a passionate fervour, but then, as the triumph of his opinions diminished his interest in debate, he wanted no part in being just another standard-bearer. On this unique occasion when he took a stand in factional conflict, he gave proof of convictions, rarely revealed, that were absolute, unyielding and tenaciously held.

In 1832, shortly after his arrival in Paris, in music as in literature a new school was formed and young talents appeared that brilliantly cast off the yoke of ancient prescriptions. The political agitation of the first years following the 'July Revolution', having scarcely diminished, was fervently carried over into matters of art and literature that captured the attention of many minds. Romanticism was the order of the day and it was furiously fought over, for and against. There could be no truce between those who would not admit that art could be different from what it had been in the past, and those who wanted the artist to be free to choose the form and mould it to his feeling, each different mode of feeling sanctioning a different mode of expression. Those wedded to the past believed in the existence of a permanent form whose perfection represented absolute beauty, and judged each work from this predetermined point of view, wishing to enclose in a symmetrical framework the inspiration of dissimilar personalities and natures. In their insistence that the Great Masters had attained supreme perfection in art, they left to succeeding artists no glory other than in imitation, denying them even the hope of equalling them since the perfecting of technique can never match original invention. Their opponents denied that beauty could have a fixed and absolute form. They argued that the many forms that had appeared in the history of art were like tents pitched on the route to an ideal: temporary stopping places that genius reaches from epoch to epoch and which its heirs must go beyond. They claimed for artists the freedom of creating their own style, accepting no rule other than one that springs from the direct relation between sentiment and form, the one suited to the other (existing models, however admirable, having not exhausted the emotional range that art possesses, or all the forms that it can use). Aiming beyond the excellence of form, they sought it only to the extent that its perfection was indispensable to the complete revelation of feeling, being aware that feeling is damaged if form, like a veil, dims its radiance. Thus they subordinated craftsmanship to poetic inspiration, calling upon patience and genius to create that form which satisfied the demands of inspiration. They

Chapter 5

reproached their conservative opponents for subjecting inspiration to Procrustean torture,[8] for insisting that certain feelings could not be expressed in predetermined form, thus depriving art of works that would have tried to introduce new feelings in new forms – feelings that arise from the ever-progressing development of the human spirit as well as from the material resources of art.

Those who saw the flames of talent consume the old worm-eaten scaffolds affiliated themselves to the musical school of which Berlioz was the most gifted, most courageous and most daring representative. Chopin joined wholeheartedly and became one of those who most resolutely freed himself from the formulas of conventional style while rejecting the charlatanism that might have replaced the old abuses with new ones.

Throughout the several years that this campaign for Romanticism lasted, with experiments that were masterstrokes, Chopin remained as firm in his predilections as in his antipathies. He wasted no time on those who were not, in his view, sincerely devoted to progress, those who, in pursuing transient success by merely dazzling an audience, exploited art for professional profit. He respectfully broke the ties he had made when they became annoyingly restrictive, when he felt moored too close to the shore by ropes already rotted. He stubbornly refused to form ties with young artists whose success, to his mind, had been exaggerated. He never gave the least praise to anything that was not a conquest for art, or which was not a serious idea worthy of the artist. He did not wish to be lionised or privileged by the manoeuvrings and inducements proffered by the leaders of musical factions. He rejected the rivalries, encroachments and degradations of style found in the different branches of art, together with all negotiations and manoeuvrings freighted with trickery and compromises. And in refusing outside support for the reception of his works, he often said that their beauties were enough to ensure their appreciation and made no effort to expedite their immediate acceptance.

Chopin gave to our trials and struggles, then full of uncertainty and scepticism, the support of a calm unwavering conviction, a stability of character equal to the challenge of weariness and deceit, a rare immutability of will, as well as valuable works that the cause could appropriate. He combined his boldness with such charm, restraint and learning that he was justified in believing in his own much-admired genius. The exhaustive study he had made, the reflective habits of his youth, the worship of classic beauty in which he was raised prevented his energies from being dissipated in miserable groping and partial success – as has happened to more than one champion of new ideas. His studious patience in fashioning and polishing his works sheltered him from those critics who seize upon any negligence or oversight. Trained early in rigorous rules, even writing beautiful works in which they were adhered to, he discarded them only after careful reflection. He constantly moved forward by virtue of his principles, free of exaggeration and compromise, and willingly abandoned theoretical methods to obtain the right result. Less occupied with academic disputes and terminology than in winning the argument with the finished work, he avoided personal enmities and distressing compromises.

Along with an approach that was modern, Chopin worshipped art with the same reverence as the early masters of the Middle Ages. For him, as for them, art was a beautiful and holy vocation, and like them he was proud of his calling and brought to it a religious devotion. This feeling was revealed at the hour of his death in a significant detail that is best explained by a Polish custom. By a practice that continues there, although now falling into disuse, the dying often choose the garments in which they wish to be buried and which some have prepared long in advance: thus are their dearest, most intimate, thoughts expressed for the last time. Chopin, who among the greatest of contemporary artists had given the fewest concerts, nevertheless wished to be buried in the clothes he had worn on such occasions. A deep and instinctive feeling, flowing from the inexhaustible passion for his art, without doubt dictated this last wish as he scrupulously fulfilled the last duties of a Christian and left behind all things temporal. Long before the approach of death he had linked his love and faith in art immortality, so that as he lay in his coffin he affirmed one last time with a silent symbolism the conviction that he kept intact throughout his life. He died faithful to himself, worshipping art for all its mystical greatness and revelations.

As we have said, while shunning the whirl of society, Chopin focused his concern and affections on his family and the acquaintances of his youth, close and uninterrupted links of which he took great care. His sister Louise [Ludwika] was especially dear to him since a certain resemblance in their ways of thinking and feeling bound them closely together. She frequently came from Warsaw to Paris to see him, finally coming to spend the last three months of her brother's life, surrounding him with her devoted care.

Chapter 5

Chopin maintained a regular correspondence with members of his family, but only with them. One of his peculiarities was to write letters to no others as if he had vowed never to write to strangers. It was curious to see him resort to all kinds of expedients to avoid penning even the most insignificant note. Many a time he preferred to cross Paris from end to end to decline an invitation to dinner or to convey some trivial information in order to spare himself the trouble of writing a few lines. Consequently, his handwriting remained unknown to most of his friends. It is said that he sometimes broke this habit for his beautiful countrywomen, some of whom possess several notes written in Polish. These lapses may be attributed to the pleasure he took in speaking his own language, always using it with the people of his own country and loving to translate its most expressive idioms. Like Slavs in general, he had very good French which, because of his French origin, had been taught to him with care, yet he was prejudiced against it and criticised it for being unpleasant on the ear and cold in essence.

Chopin's opinion of the French language is quite prevalent among Poles who, although speaking the language with great facility, complain of the impossibility of rendering in it ethereal and shimmering nuances of thought. They believe that French sometimes lacks majesty, sometimes passion and sometimes gracefulness. If they are asked the meaning of a line of verse or speech that is cited in Polish, their reply to the foreigner is invariably: 'Oh, it's untranslatable!' Then follows an explanation as to why all the subtleties, innuendo and opposites are to be found in untranslatable words. We can cite several examples that lead us to assume that Polish has the advantage of conceptualising abstract nouns and that, as it evolved through the poetic genius of the nation it was able to establish a striking correlation between ideas through etymologies, derivations and synonyms. The result is like a coloured reflection, light and shade, cast upon all expressions that, one might say, vibrate in the mind like a musical third that modulates thought into a major or minor chord. The richness of the language always permits the choice of tonality. However, this very richness can be a difficulty and it may be that the prevalent use of foreign languages in Poland is due to laziness in mastering the diction demanded by a language so full of sudden depths and powerful concision. Ill-defined thoughts cannot be compressed in the strong framework of its grammar. Because of the character of the language, Polish literature shows a greater number of masterpieces in proportion to the number of authors than in any other language; he who ventures to use it must already have mastered it.⁹

In his relations with his parents, Chopin displayed a delightful graciousness. Not content with corresponding with them almost exclusively, he took advantage of his stay in Paris to obtain for them a thousand surprises, novelties, trifles and all kinds of small pretty things whose charm lay in their novelty. He looked for anything that he thought would be well received in Warsaw, and wished these gifts to be kept by their recipients. For his part, he set great store by all the proofs of their affection for him, and receiving news, or some sign of their remembrance of him, was always a cause for celebration. And although he shared it with no one, one was aware of the fuss that he made of all that they sent him: the least gift was precious to him and he did not allow anyone to use such items, being visibly upset if anyone even touched them.

Material elegance was as natural to him as that of the mind, this trait being revealed as much in the objects with which he surrounded himself as in his refined manners. He loved flowers and, without the dazzling luxury that some Parisian celebrities of that epoch decorated their apartments, knew how to strike a balance, in this regard as well as in his dress, between too much and too little and draw an instinctive line of perfect propriety.

Keeping free of others in time, thought and action, he often preferred the company of women, since they were less likely to involve him in continuing contact. He would willingly spend whole evenings playing blind man's bluff with young people, telling them little stories that made them laugh with that rippling laughter of youth that is sweeter than the nightingale's song. He enjoyed the countryside and the life of the chateau and was ingenious in varying its delights and increasing its enjoyments. He also loved to work there, and several of his best works perhaps contain the memory of these, his happiest days.

CHAPTER 6

CHOPIN WAS BORN IN 1810 in Zelazowa-Wola, near Warsaw. Unlike most children, he had no memory of his age, the date of his birth being fixed in his mind only by a watch given to him in 1820 by Madame Catalani which bore the inscription: 'Madame Catalani to Frédéric Chopin, aged ten years'.[1] Perhaps the artist's premonition gave the child a glimpse of his future! His boyhood was unremarkable and probably unfolded calmly, except that he was a frail and sickly child and his family's attention was concentrated on his health. It was from this time that he acquired his friendly manner, charm and stoicism in the face of suffering, all of which stemmed from a desire to allay the anxieties he caused to others. In these early years there were no signs of precocity or of a future superiority of soul, of mind or of talent. As a child he was seen as suffering and smiling, always patient and cheerful, and, being neither moody nor morose, others were content to cherish his good qualities, believing that he opened his heart without reserve and shared the secrets of all his thoughts. Yet there are souls who, when young, are like rich travellers brought by chance among simple herdsmen who, heaping small gifts upon their hosts, astonish them and spread happiness in the midst of their poor simplicity. Such souls give as much affection, perhaps more than they receive from those who surround them, except that, although the recipient is satisfied, they have given little, and have lavished but few of their treasures.

The environment that Chopin knew from an early age, and in which he grew up, was a soft yet solid cradle; close-knit, calm and industrious, it provided him with the sweetest and dearest models of simplicity, piety and honour. Domestic virtues and religious observance, pious charity and inherent modesty, surrounded him with an atmosphere so pure that his imagination acquired the velvet tenderness of plants that are never exposed to the dust of busy highways.

He began to learn music at the early age, beginning to receive formal instruction when he was nine. Soon he was entrusted to

Żywny, a passionate disciple of Sebastian Bach, who guided his studies for many years in accordance with the strictest classicism.[2] It must not be assumed that, when he embraced a musical career, no misplaced pride or lure of fantastic prospects dazzled his eyes and excited the hopes of his family. He was made to study seriously and conscientiously so that he would become a resourceful master without any thought of the fame that might flow from his lessons and hard work.

When still young, Chopin was placed in one of Warsaw's leading colleges as a result of the generous and discriminating patronage that Prince Antoine Radziwiłł, a distinguished man and artist, extended to the arts and especially to young talent.[3] Prince Radziwiłł did not cultivate music as a mere dilettante but as a remarkable composer. His fine score of *Faust*, published some years ago and regularly performed by the Singakademie in Berlin, captures the poem's essence and is superior to any other setting. By supplementing the very limited means of Chopin's family, the prince, presented the boy with the priceless gift of a good education, and no part of it was neglected. From Chopin's entry into college to the completion of his studies, the Prince, whose enlightened outlook grasped the demands of an artistic career, supported him through the mediation of a friend, M. Antoine Korzuchowski, who maintained contact with the composer until the latter's death.

In speaking of this period of his life, we have the pleasure of quoting some charming lines, more applicable to him than other pages in which his character is traced and distorted.[4]

> Gentle, sensitive, and exquisite in all things, he had at fifteen all the charms of adolescence combined with a mature dignity. He was delicate both in body and in mind. But the lack of muscular development gave him a beauty, an exceptional facial loveliness that had, as it were, neither age or sex. It was not the bold and masculine appearance of a descendant of an ancient race of magnates, who knew nothing but drinking, hunting and warfare, neither was it the effeminate prettiness of a rosy cherub. It was more like the idealised creatures with which the poetry of the Middle Ages adorned Christian churches: a beautiful angel, with a face like a sorrowing lady, pure and slight in form like an young Olympian god and, to crown all, an expression both tender and severe, chaste and passionate.[5]
>
> That was the core of his being. Nothing was more pure and, at the same time, more exalted than his thoughts, nothing more constant, more exclusive, more intensely devoted, than his affections. . . . He only

Chapter 6

understood what was similar to himself. . . . All else existed for him only as a kind of annoying dream, which he tried to escape from while living in the real world. Always lost in his own reveries, he disliked reality. As a child he could never touch a sharp instrument without hurting himself; and, as an adult, he could never deal with another person different from himself without colliding with a living contradiction.[6]

He was saved from constant resentment by a voluntary and later inveterate habit of never seeing or hearing anything that generally displeased him unless it touched him personally. People who did not think as he did were as phantoms in his eyes and, since he had charming manners, a courteous grace could hide cold disdain, even unconquerable dislike.[7]

He never spent an hour of expansiveness without compensating for it with many more of withdrawal, the moral causes of which were too slight and too subtle to be seen by the naked eye. A microscope was needed to read his soul where so little of the light of the living ever penetrated.[8]

It is remarkable that such a character should have had friends. And yet he did, not only the friends of his mother who regarded him as a worthy son of a noble woman, but also friends of his own age, who loved him dearly and who were loved by him in return. . . . He had formed a high ideal of friendship. In the illusions of his youth, he believed that he and his friends, having been brought up nearly in the same manner and with the same principles, would never change their opinions, and would never fundamentally disagree about anything.[9]

He was outwardly so affectionate, as a result of his good education and natural grace that he had the gift of pleasing even those who did not know him personally. His handsome face was much in his favour; his physical frailty made him attractive to women; and his rich intellect, together with his gentle and flattering conversation, won him the attention of educated men. Even men made of less refined stuff liked him for his exquisite manner; this pleased them because, in their simplicity, they never imagined it was merely an exercise in duty in which sympathy was not involved.[10]

Had such people been able to read his nature, they would have said he was more pleasant than loving and, as far as they were concerned, this would have been true. How could they have known that his real attachments were so intense, so deep and so unshakeable?[11]

In everyday life he was delightful company. He was always graciously kind and when he acknowledged others' kindness it was with a deep emotion that repaid friendship with interest.[12]

Each day, he was prone to imagine that he was dying and would respond to the concern of a friend with this thought in mind, hiding from him how little time he believed he had left. He possessed great outward courage and, although he did not accept the idea of approaching death with the carefree heroism of youth, he at least toyed with it with a kind of bitter pleasure.[13]

It was in this early period of his youth that he became attached to a young lady whose deep attachment to him never ceased. The tempest that tore Chopin away from his native land, leaving him like a confused and distracted bird on the branches of a foreign tree, broke off this first love and deprived him of both his country and a faithful and devoted wife. In his days of glory he was never to encounter the happiness that he had dreamed of with her. This young girl was as beautiful as she was gentle and, like one of Luini's Madonnas, her looks were full of sober tenderness.[14] She remained calm and sad, a sadness surely intensified by the knowledge that no devotion like hers ever came into the life of him she adored with the childlike submissiveness, the exclusive devotion, and that innocent and sublime abandon that transforms a woman into an angel.

Those whom nature burdens with the fatal, beautiful gifts of genius are forbidden to neglect glory for love, and are to be forgiven for imposing limits on the sacrifice of their personality. It may be that the divine emotions that flow from absolute devotion will be regretted in the presence of the most sparkling gifts of genius. There is but one means for a man to sanctify the totality of a woman's love, to acknowledge that she has uniquely shared his life, to affirm that his love has brought her what no chance lover could bring: the honour of his name and the peace of his heart.

Unexpectedly separated from Chopin, this young girl remained faithful to his memory and to all that he left behind. She devoted herself to his parents so that Chopin's father would never replace her portrait of his son (drawn in more hopeful days) with another. Many years later, we saw the pale cheeks of this sad woman slowly colour, as alabaster blushes in light when, in gazing upon this picture, her eyes met those of his father.[15]

Chopin's charming and easy-going nature ensured that he made friends in school including Prince Borys Czetwertyński and his brothers.[16] He often spent his holidays with them and their mother, the Princess Louise Czetwertyńska, who cultivated music with a true feeling for its beauties and who soon discovered the poet in the musician. Perhaps she was the first to give him the satisfaction of being

Chapter 6

understood as well as heard. The Princess was still beautiful and possessed a sympathetic mind enhanced by noble qualities, and her salon was one of the most brilliant and select in Warsaw. It was there that Chopin often met the most distinguished women of the capital, some of them fascinating beauties of Europe-wide fame, at a time when Warsaw was renowned for the splendour, elegance and grace of its society. Through the Princess's mediation he had the honour of being presented at the home of Princess de Lowicz where he was introduced to Countess Zamoyska, Princess Radziwiłł and Princess Thérèse Jabłonowska, enchantresses all who were surrounded by many other less illustrious beauties.[17]

While he was still young he often accompanied their dancing from the piano. It was at these parties, which might be called fairy gatherings, that he discovered in the excitement of the dance the secrets of impassioned and tender hearts. He could easily read those souls who were drawn to his youth through attraction and friendship and from them learned what comprised his nation's poetic ideal: a leaven of rose-paste, gunpowder and angel tears. When his fingers casually ran over the keys, suddenly striking some touching chords, he saw how furtive tears ran down the cheeks of smitten young girls and neglected young wives, and how too were moistened the eyes of the young men, passionate and jealous of glory. Did not some young beauty, having asked him to play a simple prelude, lean her exquisite arm upon the instrument to support her dreaming head and let him guess in her look what song her heart was singing? Did not some group, made up of playful nymphs, to get from him some waltz of giddying speed, surround him with smiles and teach him how to mingle with their gaiety? There, in the mazurka, he saw displayed the decorous grace of his magnificent countrywomen, and thereafter kept a deathless memory of their glamour and discretion.

Chopin would sometimes recall, casually and with the quiet emotion that characterises the memories of youth, how he first understood all the feelings contained in the melodies and rhythms of national dances: when he saw exquisite sprites, brilliantly adorned, at a magical celebration, quickening, blinding and discouraging love. He also recalled that often, however good an orchestra might be, the dancers glided less rapidly over the floor, their laugh less resounding, their looks less radiant, their fatigue felt sooner than on those evenings when he had improvised the dance and electrified his audience. He explained that when he electrified them it was by producing in sound what he had caught of the passionate whisperings of their hearts, comparable to the fraxinella, its flowers wreathed in a vapour both subtle and inflammable.[18] He sensed the swarm of emotions that flitted through their souls, a pulsation and agitation that never disturbed the beautiful harmony of visible grace. Thus did he learn to relish and prize noble manners when allied to an intensity of feeling that preserved refinement from blandness, convention from tyranny, good taste from rigidity.

These early glimpses into a world where formality did not conceal an emotional paralysis led Chopin to believe that formality, convention and propriety, instead of being a mask of uniformity, served to subdue passions without stifling them. That these qualities removed perverting crudeness, debased expression, vulgar manners, casual anger and tiring enthusiasm, and taught the *lovers of the unattainable* to combine the virtues revealed by knowledge of evil with those that cause *it* [evil] *to be forgotten when addressing the object of love*. As these early visions of youth took root in his memory and imagination they gained in grace, charm and glamour, so that no opposing reality could destroy their secret fascination. They reinforced his repugnance of that freedom of action, the tyrannous brutality of caprice, the determination to drain dry the cup of imagination, and the pursuit of all the dangers and confusions found in that strange and ever-changing milieu: the bohemian life.

Many a time has a poet or artist appeared who embodies a poetic sense of a people, or of an era, representing in his works that which contemporaries can only aspire to realise in own creations. Chopin was that poet for his country and for his era since he embodied in his imagination, and represented in his poetic genius, the feelings that were then most widespread and most intrinsic to his nation. Poland has given birth to many bards, some of whom rank among the foremost in the world. Now, more than ever, its writers are exploring the most remarkable and glorious aspects of its history and spirit, as well as bringing out the unusual and colourful aspects of its landscape and customs. But Chopin, differing from them in having formed no preconceived plan, surpassed them perhaps in originality. He did not want, nor did he seek, such a result, he created no ideal *a priori*. He did not recall the patriotic glories of Poland to live in the past; rather he understood and sang of present-day love and tears without analysing them in advance. He neither studied nor strove to be a national musician and it is possible that he would be shocked to be regarded as one. Like all true national poets he sang without a fixed plan, or predetermined choice, whatever inspiration spontaneously dictated to him. Consequently, effortlessly in this way, the most idealised emotions appeared in his music, feelings that had enlivened his childhood and embellished his youth. Thus the ideal, the real and truly existing ideal of his people, flowed from his pen, an ideal which could be approached by everyone generally as well as by each person individually in their own way. Without special intent he collected, in luminous bundles, sensations that were confusedly felt throughout his country, feelings that were scattered in all hearts, but only vaguely acknowledged by a few. Is not this gift of reproducing in a poetic format, and with an international appeal, the blurred outlines of feeling scattered among compatriots that which identifies national artists?

Since there are now those who, with good reason, are carefully collecting indigenous melodies of different lands, it seems to us interesting to devote some attention to how artists respond when they are especially inspired by national genius. Until now there have been few distinctive compositions that stand apart from the two great schools of German and Italian music. But it may be that with the development of which art seems capable in our century (perhaps analogous to the glorious era of the *cinquecento* painters), artists [*auteurs*] will emerge whose works will be marked by an originality drawn from differences of national character, race and climate. It is likely that in music, as in the other arts, the influences of country and nation on great masters will increase with the result that the spirit of the people, more complete, more poetically true and more interesting to study, will influence its future, rather than the crude, misconceived and hesitant jottings of popular inspiration.

Chopin will be ranked among the foremost musicians who thus individualised in themselves the poetic sense of a whole nation – but not just because he adopted the rhythm of polonaises, mazurkas and cracoviennes[19] and called many of his works by such names. Had he limited himself simply to increasing their number, he would have repeated the identical formula, the pattern and memory of the same thing, producing tedious replicas that would merely serve to sustain forms that had become boring. If he is to be considered as an essentially Polish poet, it is because he used form to express the manner of feeling prevalent in his country, and because these feelings are found in all the forms in which he composed. His preludes, nocturnes and, above all, his scherzos and concertos, that is both his shortest and his longest compositions, are all to varying degrees filled with the same sensibility, modified and varied in a thousand ways, but always the one and the same. Chopin, an eminently subjective composer, gave his works the same life, animating all his music with his own spirit. Thus all his compositions have a unity, and their beauties (like their defects) always reflect the same emotional world: a fundamental requirement for any poet if his songs are to stir as one the hearts of his people.

We should have liked to convey here, by analogous word or picture, a clearer impression of Chopin's sensibility, both exquisite and irritable, which is peculiar to ardent and inconstant hearts, as well as to haughty and wounded natures. We cannot flatter ourselves that we have imparted the ethereal, scented flame within the limitations of the printed word, could this even be done. Do not words always seem bland, petty, cold and dry after the strong and suave excitement that the other arts can provide? Is it not said, with good reason, *that of all the ways to express feeling, the word is the most inadequate?* Similarly, we cannot flatter ourselves that we have achieved in these lines the delicate brushstrokes needed to reproduce what Chopin depicted with such inimitable lightness of touch: for there all is subtle, even the sources of anger and rage. There frank and simple impulses disappear because they have all been passed through the sieve of a fertile, ingenious and demanding imagination: all demand insight to be understood and delicacy to be described. Thus Chopin, with infinite art and remarkable taste, became an artist of the first order. It is only through long and patient study, by the constant pursuit of the many changes of thought that a full understanding and admiration is gained. Only then does it become clear with what talent he made his thought tangible.

Chopin was so absolutely and uniquely steeped in feelings, the best of which he believed he had cherished since his youth, that he wanted to confide them uniquely to his art – but only within his own singular, unchanging artistic perspective. He uniquely sought in art's great masterpieces only what corresponded to his own nature. He was pleased with what was agreeable, but rendered scant justice to what was not. Combining in himself the incompatible qualities of passion and grace, he possessed great judgement and impartiality, and scarcely paused before even the greatest beauties and highest skills when they offended any aspect of his poetic conception. Whatever admiration he entertained for Beethoven's works, certain passages

Chapter 6

seemed to him too roughly carved, their structure too muscular, their anger too roaring, and their passion to close to disaster. His taste found the lion marrow that is found in every phase too weighty, and the seraphic Raphaelesque contours that appear in this great genius's powerful creations were to him at times almost painful in their lacerating contrast.

Although he acknowledged the charm of some of Schubert's melodies, he unwillingly listened to those with melodic lines too sharp for his ear, where feeling is stripped naked, where one can hear, as it were, the twitching of flesh and the cracking of bones in sorrow's embrace. All harshness repelled him. In music, in literature and in the conduct of life, all that verged on the melodramatic was torture for him. He was repelled by the unbridled and frenzied side of Romanticism, and could not endure its confused effects and delirious excesses.

> He liked Shakespeare but with strong reservations, finding his characters too lifelike and their speech too earthy. Rather he preferred the fusion of the epic and the lyric that leaves the sad details of humanity in shadow. For this reason he spoke little and rarely listened, only wishing to express his own thoughts, and only accepting those of others after they had attained a certain refinement.[20]

His nature, always so self-controlled and full of sensitive reserve, cherished those powers of suggestion so dear to poets, and was vexed, even scandalised, by all that left nothing to be grasped beyond the obvious. Had he been forced to express his own views upon this subject, we believe he would have confessed that his taste allowed him to express feelings only when most were left to be intuited. If he felt that the *classical* [*classique*] in art was too restrictive for him; if he refused to be manacled by conventional systems; if he fought against the confines of a square cage, it was so that he might soar and sing like a lark never to swoop down from the heights. Likewise, with equal determination did he stubbornly refuse to plunge into forest glens to experience their howling and wailing, nor would he explore terrible deserts to trace paths that the treacherous winds so quickly and so mockingly sweep away.

Chopin was as displeased with all that in Italian music is so simple, so lucid, so glittering, and so devoid of erudition, as he was with all that in German art is stamped with powerful, yet vulgar, energy. He once remarked of Schubert, 'the sublime is corrupted when followed by the trivial or commonplace'. Among composers for the piano, Hummel[21] was one he reread with the most pleasure while, in his eyes, Mozart was the ideal, the supreme poet, because he rarely crossed the line that separates refinement from vulgarity. He loved in Mozart precisely that for which the latter's father, having attended a performance of *Idomeneo*, reproached his son: 'You were wrong in putting nothing in it for idiots'. Papageno's cheerfulness charmed his own; Tamino's love and mysterious ordeals seemed worthy subjects; Zerlina and Masetto amused him with their refined naivety; and he understood Donna Anna's revenge because it cloaked her mourning in deeper grief. And yet his questing after purity, his dread of the commonplace, was such that even in *Don Giovanni*, an immortal masterpiece, he found passages of which, in our hearing, he disapproved, although his worship of Mozart remained undiminished (if saddened) by his reservations. Although he succeeded in forgetting what repelled him, he found acceptance impossible. Did he not in this respect suffer grievously from an instinctive, irrational and implacable superiority, so that no persuasion or effort could make him indifferent towards what he disliked even to the point of idiosyncrasy?

When his school years were over, and he had finished his rigorous study of harmony with Professor Josef Elsner, who taught him to be exacting towards himself and to value patience and hard work, his parents urged him to travel so that he might hear fine performances of the great masterpieces. For this purpose he briefly visited many German cities, and it was while he was away on one of these short excursions from Warsaw in 1830 that the revolution of 29 November broke out.

Forced to remain in Vienna, Chopin gave some concerts. Yet during that winter, the Viennese public, usually so intelligent and quick to grasp subtlety in performance and musical thought, showed so little interest in him that he failed to produce the sensation there he had a right to expect. He therefore left the city with the intention of going to London, stopping in Paris where he intended to stay only briefly, even adding the words 'passing through Paris' on his passport stamped for England, a phrase that summed up his future at that time. Years afterwards when he was perfectly acclimatised and naturalised in France, he would laughingly say, 'I am only passing through'.

On his arrival in Paris he gave several concerts that at once secured him the deepest admiration of high society and of young artists. We remember his first appearance at the Pleyel salon, where the most rapturous applause seemed insufficient to express our enchantment

Chapter 6

when confronted with a talent that was launching a new era of poetic feeling with such exciting innovations in the substance of his art.

Unlike most young newcomers, Chopin was not corrupted for a moment by the intoxication of success, but accepted it without pride or false modesty, displaying none of the puerile vanity flaunted by successful upstarts. All his compatriots in Paris gave him the most eager and affectionate welcome. He was an intimate at the house of Prince Czartoryski, Countess Plater, Mme de Komar and her daughters, the Princess de Beauveau – and Countess Delphine Potocka whose beauty, together with her indescribable spiritual grace, made her one of the most admired sovereigns of high society.[22] He dedicated to the latter his *Second Concerto*, which contains the Adagio that we mentioned earlier. The ethereal beauty of the Countess, together with her talent and her enchanting voice, drew from him the most admiring fascination. It was her voice that was the last that he was to hear, mingling for him the sweetest earthly sounds with the first chords of the heavenly choir.

Chopin mixed with many young Poles: Fontana, Orda, who seemed to command the future (but was killed in Algiers aged twenty), Counts Plater, Grzymała, Ostrowski, Szembeck, Prince Lubomirski and others.[23] Polish families who subsequently arrived in Paris were anxious to become acquainted with him, and he increasingly favoured moving in a large circle mostly comprised of his compatriots. Through them, he not only remained informed about all that was happening in his homeland but also maintained a kind of musical correspondence with it. He loved to be shown the airs or new songs that Polish visitors brought with them to Paris and, when the words of these airs pleased him, he would often add a new melody to them – thus popularising them rapidly in his homeland without the composer's name ever being known. As the number of these melodies, solely inspired by the heart, grew, Chopin often thought of collecting them for publication in his last years. But he no longer had the opportunity to do so and they remain lost or scattered, like the fragrance of flowers that grow in inhospitable places some day to perfume the path of an unknown traveller. In Poland we heard some of the melodies attributed to him and truly worthy of his talent, but who today would try to sort out the poet's inspirations from those of his people?

For a long time, Chopin held himself aloof from the most sought-after celebrities of Paris since their raucous followers repelled him. For his part, he aroused less curiosity than they, since his character and habits had more genuine originality than eccentricity. He had caustic ripostes for those who impudently wished to exploit his talent; as on one occasion when, after he had left the dining room, an ill-advised host, who had naively promised his guests, as a rare dessert, a piece played by Chopin, pointed him towards an open piano. At first Chopin simply refused, but wearied by unacceptable persistence, remarked in a muffled and sarcastic tone of voice: 'Ah! sir, but I have scarcely dined!'

CHAPTER 7

B Y 1836 MME SAND HAD PUBLISHED not only *Indiana*, *Valentine* and *Jacques*, but also *Lélia*, a poem of which she later remarked, 'If I regret having written it, it is because I could not write it now. If I could return to the same state of mind it would be a great relief to start all over again.'[1] Indeed, to Mme Sand the novel's watercolours must have seemed insipid after she had wielded the sculptor's hammer and chisel in cutting Lélia's huge statue with its sweeping lines, bold relief and sinewy muscles, with such seductive monumentality. As we contemplate Lélia she moves us almost painfully; in contrast to Pygmalion,[2] she seems a living Galatea,[3] rich in soft impulses, sensually alert and full of the tenderness with which the artist lovingly imparted to the stone to augment and immortalise her beauty. Thus is nature transformed into art.

Dark and olive-skinned Lélia! Thou hast walked lonely paths, as solemn as Lara, as broken as Manfred, as rebellious as Cain, yet more ferocious, more pitiless and more inconsolable than they.[4] Thou hast never found a man's heart sufficiently feminine to love thee, or to pay homage to thy virile charms with blind yet confident submission, or to allow itself to be protected by thy Amazonian strength![5] Like those woman-heroes, thou hast been brave and eager for battle; like them, thou hast not been afraid to expose the satin loveliness of thy face to wind or sun, or to strengthen thy limbs through endurance! Like them too, thou hast had to strap on a cuirass that has cut and bloodied thy bosom which, lovely as life and as secret as the grave, man adores when his heart is its only and impenetrable shield!

Mme Sand blunted her chisel in polishing Lélia's image, with its nobility and disdain, its anguished glance and locks full of electric life, its fine brow and haughty smile of Medusa.[6] An image fashioned with an infinite art to compensate for what her heroine had repudiated: the supreme greatness of self-abnegation in love, which Goethe called 'the eternal feminine' (*das Ewigweibliche*),[7] that greatness of a love that pre-exists all its joys and survives all its sorrows.[8] And when she had finished, Mme Sand searched in vain for another form that could express the feelings that lacerated her unsatisfied soul. In her *Lettres d'un voyageur* she describes the quivering apathy and aching heaviness that seizes an artist when, having captured in a work the feeling that inspired him, his imagination remains under its influence without finding another form for its idealisation. Byron understood the poet's distress when, in *Tasso* he makes his hero shed the bitterest tears, not for his prison, his chains, his physical suffering or the degradation of men but for his finished epic and his world of thought which, slipping away, made him at last aware of the terrible reality of his plight.[9]

At this time, Mme Sand often heard Chopin described as a truly exceptional artist by one of his musician friends, one of the many who had enthusiastically greeted him upon his arrival at Paris. She heard praise of his talent and even more of his poetic genius, and came to know and admire his works for their amorous sweetness. She was especially struck by the wealth of feeling that permeated his music and distinguished his noble expressiveness. About the same time too, some of Chopin's compatriots spoke to her enthusiastically of the women of Poland with a fervour intensified by the recent memory of their sacrifices during the last war.[10] She glimpsed in their stories, and in Chopin's poetic inspiration, an ideal of love that worshipped woman. She believed that there, totally independent and completely equal, her role was to match the magical powers of the Peri[11] and to become involved with him. She did not sense what a long chain of suffering and silence, of patience and forbearance, of indulgence and courageous perseverance, had created his proud and resigned ideal. Admirable yet sad to behold, it resembled those plants with rose-coloured corollas whose stems, intertwining in a network of long and numerous strands, give life to ruins, destined by Nature to embellish crumbling stones: with what inexhaustible generosity and ingenuity are beautiful veils thrown over decay in human affairs![12]

Instead of fashioning his marvellous ideas in porphyry and marble, like massive caryatids casting their thought from on high, Chopin stripped them of all weight and suspended them in the clouds like palaces of air. Impressed by such expressions of lightness, Mme Sand was thus more attracted to the ideal that, she believed, they embodied. Although she had the arm of a sculptor, her hand was delicate enough to trace the most delicate reliefs that leave only the lightest trace in the stone. No stranger to the supernatural world, she was

Chapter 7

like a favoured daughter of Nature who was capable of unloosing her garments to reveal all the caprice, charm and freedom of beauty.[13] She had an awareness of the most imperceptible graces, for she knew the colours of butterfly wings and had studied the marvellous symmetry of the fern as it enfolded the wild strawberry in its canopy. She had listened to murmuring streams in water meadows where the hissing of the love-viper may be heard, and had followed will-o'-the-wisps as they flashed over field and fen, and imagined the wild places to which they drew the flagging traveller. She had listened to the concerts given by the cicada and its friends in the stubble of the fields, and knew all the inhabitants of the winged republic of the woods recognising them by their plumage, their chattering, and their plaintive calls. She also well knew the softness and splendour of the lily, as well as the despair of Geneviève, the maiden in love with flowers.[14]

In her dreams Mme Sand was visited by 'unknown friends' who came to keep her company 'when she was distressed upon a desolate shore' and on to whose 'large and laden boat' she rushed to sail for unknown shores:

> [to] that land of chimeras that makes real life seem like a half-forgotten dream to those enamoured from childhood of great shells of pearl, [to] those islands where all are young and beautiful. . . . Where the men and women, crowned with flowers, their hair floating on their shoulders, . . . hold cups and strangely shaped harps, have songs and voices that are not of this world, [. . . and] love each other with a divine love. . . . Where perfumed fountains play in silver basins [. . . and] blue roses grow in Chinese vases. . . . Where the views are enchanted . . . and where they walk barefoot on moss as smooth as velvet carpet and run and sing while wandering among the fragrant shrubs![15]

She knew these 'unknown friends' so well that after they had appeared 'she could not think of them without trembling all day'. She was an initiate into the world of Hoffmann,[16] and the fantastic had no secret that she did not share.

Mme Sand thus became anxious to know Chopin because he could flee 'to regions that, although impossible to describe, must exist somewhere on earth or on some distant planet that sheds a lovely light on the woods at the setting of the moon'.[17] To her he was a being who no longer wished to leave those regions or bring his heart and imagination back to this world. Wearied by Lélia's burdensome vision and the dream of an impossible fashioned from earthly materials, she wanted to know that artist who was a lover of an impossible so intangible and so close to the lands beyond the moon. Alas! Although those regions are beyond our contaminated atmosphere, they are not free of the world's desolating sadness. Those who go there see not only burning suns but also suns that are burnt out. The noblest stars of the Pleiades vanish there, while others fall, like drops of shining dew, into nothingness. There, the soul, contemplating these ethereal savannahs, this blue Sahara, with its shifting and transient oases, becomes accustomed to an unbroken and inconsolable melancholy. This sadness engulfs and absorbs it, like the still waters of a lake, its surface mirroring the shore while its deadly stillness remains unchanged. Such melancholy can stifle even the most intense happiness:

> With an exhaustion that always goes with such stress of the soul; . . . it shows the inadequacy of human speech for the first time to those who have studied it so much, and used it so well . . . . It travels, far from material and militant instincts, lost in space and in the immensity of its adventures, far above the clouds . . . . Where the earth looks beautiful no more, and where only the sky can be seen . . . where reality is no longer imagined with the poetic sensibility of the author of *Waverley*, but where, the poem itself being idealised, the infinite is peopled with its own creations as in *Manfred*.[18]

Did Mme Sand sense the incurable melancholy, obdurate will and imperious exclusivity that accompanies contemplation and controls the imagination that pursues dreams divorced from all reality? Did she sense what might happen when tender affection is misconstrued as supreme attachment and absolute devotion? To understand the mysteries of such intense personalities it is necessary to have an instinctive reticence, since they are like flowers that close their petals at the first hint of a chill breeze, unfolding themselves only in the warming rays of the sun. Such natures have been called *rich through exclusion*, in contrast to those that are *rich through exuberance*, as Mme Sand observed: 'when they meet and mingle they can never fuse, but one must consume the other, leaving nothing but ashes behind'. Ah! there are natures like that of the frail musician whose days we recollect, that die in consuming themselves, unwilling and unable to live but a single life restricted to the demands of their own ideal.

Chopin at first seemed to dread Mme Sand more than other women since, like the Sibyl, she said things that others knew not how to say.[19] He avoided her and delayed meeting her, while, she, with her

Chapter 7

charming and natural nobility, was unaware of his shyness. But when she was finally presented to him and he gazed on her, his stubborn, long-held prejudice against female authors quickly vanished.

In the autumn of 1837 Chopin was attacked by a worrying illness that left him seriously debilitated, its alarming symptoms forcing him to go south to escape the rigours of winter.[20] Mme Sand, always so watchful and concerned over the ailments of her friends, would not let him go alone, since his condition needed care, and decided to go with him. They chose the island of Majorca, where the sea air and mild climate are especially beneficial for chest conditions. Although he was so weak when he left Paris that we thought he would never return, and despite the fact that his illness was prolonged and painful, he recovered there sufficiently for his health to be improved for several years.

Was it the climate alone that brought him back to life? Or did life hold for him a new fascination? Perhaps he had found a new will to live, for who can say how far the will influences our bodies? Who knows what inner force the will has in preventing decay and decline and how much it can energise weakened organs? Who in the end can say what power the spirit has over matter? How much does our imagination govern our senses, by increasing our faculties or hastening their demise, either over time or by concentrating forgotten strength in a single special moment? When the sun's rays are concentrated in the focal point of crystal, cannot one fragile spark light a celestial flame?

All the rays of happiness in Chopin's life were concentrated in that period, and is it surprising that they rekindled the flame of life which then burned at its brightest? That solitude, amidst the blue waves of the Mediterranean and shaded by lemon groves, seemed to fulfil the fervent wishes of two youthful souls who still clung to their innocent illusions and sighed for happiness on a desert isle! There Chopin breathed the air that engenders in exiles painful homesickness, and requires other souls to breathe it with us; the air of the idealised homeland to which we would gladly take the cherished one, repeating with Mignon: *'Dahin! dahin! . . . lasset uns ziehn!'* ['Thither, thither, let us go!'].[21]

Throughout his illness, Mme Sand never left Chopin's bedside for a moment. He loved her until the day he died with a love which, though losing all its joys, never lost its intensity, remaining faithful to her even when all had turned to pain:

for it seems that this fragile being was absorbed and consumed by the glow of his attachment. . . . Others seek happiness in their passions, and when they no longer find it their feelings gently subside. Yet he loved for the sake of loving and no amount of suffering could discourage him. And when love's rapture was eventually exhausted, he was incapable of cold indifference. Detachment would have been sheer physical agony for him because his passion, blissful or bitter, had become his life and he could not escape from it for a single moment.[22]

For Chopin Mme Sand never ceased to be the woman with supernatural powers who had forced back death's shadows, who had transformed his sufferings into delightful languor.

To save him from an early grave she struggled courageously with his disease. She lavished upon that instinctive and intuitive care that is a thousand times more efficacious than the remedies of science. As she nursed him she felt no fatigue, despondency or boredom. Like one of those mothers who seem to transfer some of their own strength to their sick child, neither her strength nor her humour flinched from the task. Finally, the disease yielded and:

> the morbid obsession that secretly undermined his spirit and corroded his happiness gradually disappeared as he allowed the easygoing nature and cheerful serenity of his partner to chase away his sad thoughts and gloomy foreboding, and to reinforce his mental wellbeing.[23]

Happiness succeeded dark fear as the triumphant dawn of a beautiful day succeeds a black night full of terrors. Although the vault of darkness weighs down so heavily that an imminent catastrophe seems inevitable, the despairing eye suddenly catches a glimpse of light, as if a hand is tearing away the shadows, and the first ray of hope enters the soul. Breathing is freer, as with those who, lost in a dark cavern, think they see a faint uncertain light! Yet this flickering light is the dawning day, proclaimed by freshening winds that bring a message of salvation in their pure, life-giving breezes. The fragrance of natural growth fills the air like the quickening of a hope reaffirmed, and a bird of the earliest morning begins a song that resounds in the heart as a promise for the future. Imperceptibly but unmistakably oppression lessens as the signs multiply that in this struggle between light and darkness, life and death, it is night's sorrows that will yield.

Little by little the grey dawn brightens stretching fissures of light

Chapter 7

along the horizon. Suddenly these chinks expand as day breaks through, like water overflowing the parched banks of a flooding pond. A contest then begins as the light begins to falter and clouds pile up like ridges of sand, but it breaks through again, demolishing and devouring them and, as it ascends, waves of purple give the sky a reddish glow. At that moment the dawn shines forth with a shy yet conquering grace, while the knee bends before its chaste gentleness as all terror has vanished. Rebirth is at hand!

Then objects sweep into view as from oblivion. A rose-coloured veil seems to hide them until the light grows brighter, as the delicate drapery shades into pale pink while the foreground brightens into a white and dazzling sheen.

The shining sun invades the sky, shedding its brilliance as it rises. Mists surge together, rolling from right to left like billowing curtains. Everything then breathes, lives, shouts and sings, the sounds mingling, clashing and melting into each other. Inertia gives way to movement that swirls, spreads and speeds away. The waves of the lake swell like a breast touched by love. Drops of dew, quivering like tears of tenderness, become visible as they glitter on the damp grass like diamonds waiting for the sun to paint their sparkling brilliance. In the east, the huge fan of light opens ever larger, as strips of gold, spangles of silver, fringes of violet, borders of scarlet and reflections of bronze cover it with their immense embroidery. At its centre, a vivid carmine with the transparency of ruby, shades into a burning orange as it flowers into a bouquet of flames that rises ever higher, ever hotter, ever more incandescent.

At last the god of day appears! He rises slowly, his brow adorned with luminous hair, but scarcely has he fully revealed himself than he takes, and ridding himself of all that surrounds him, takes possession of the sky, leaving earth far below.

The memory of those days on Majorca remained forever in Chopin's heart as an ecstatic experience that fate grants only once to the most favoured.

> He was no longer of this world but in an empyrean of golden clouds and perfumes, it almost seemed that his imagination, so exquisite and beautiful, was immersed in a monologue with God himself. And if, when he had thus lost all thought of self, some incident intruded from the magic lantern of the world, he felt deeply pained, as if in the midst of a sublime concert, a hurdy-gurdy blended its sharp and vulgar tones with the divine thoughts of the Great Masters.[24]

Thereafter he spoke gratefully of this period as one of the happiest of his life, admitting that he would never again find a time suffused with such female tenderness and musical inspiration. It was as if, like Linnaeus' clock, the time of day was told by the blossoming of flowers, each with a different perfume and each disclosing other beauties as they opened outwards.[25]

The fascinating regions through which the poet and the musician travelled together had more immediate impact on her imagination, while nature's beauties impressed Chopin just as strongly, but in a less clear-cut way. Although his soul trembled with the enchantment and grandeur of nature, resonating with the exquisite landscapes around him, his mind was not compelled precisely to analyse, document or pin down the source of each response. Like a true musician, he was happy to seize upon the feelings engendered by the scenes he saw, seemingly inattentive to the physical details and colourful contexts that did not resonate with his art and did not belong to his spiritualized world. Yet, his personality was such that, the more distant he was in time and place from scenes that had overwhelmed his emotions (as incense fumes envelop a censer), the more vividly the shapes and outlines of places and situations stood out in his memory. In the succeeding years, he spoke with great feeling of these memories of Majorca. But at the time he did not reflect on his happiness, rather letting it enfold him as do we all in childhood when we surrender to nature's influence only to find that we can recall each object in detail long after we see it no more.

Moreover, why should Chopin have paid close attention to the sights of Spain that provided the setting for his poetic happiness, could he not revisit them (and find them still lovelier) in the inspired descriptions of his travelling companion?[26] Was he not returned to them by her impassioned talent, in the same way that everything becomes as a flame seen through red stained-glass windows. Was this admirable nurse not also a great artist? What a rare and marvellous combination! If nature combined in a woman brilliant intelligence, with the deepest tenderness and devotion (wherein lies her true and irresistible power and mystery), then the flames of imagination mingling with the purity of the heart would revive the miracle of Greek fire which skims the waves without being extinguished, adding its rich purple to the sky-blue beauty of the water.[27]

Is it possible for genius to acquire the splendours of the heart, the unconditional sacrifices of the past and the future, as courageous as

Chapter 7

they are mysterious, that surrendering of self, constant and persistent, which entitles tenderness to be called devotion? Does not the power of genius have rightful demands, and is not the rightful power of woman to renounce all demands? Can the royal purple and burning flames of genius ever float upon the cloudless azure of a woman's destiny?

CHAPTER 8

CHOPIN'S HEALTH, PASSING THROUGH various phases, declined steadily after 1840 despite the respite provided each summer by weeks spent in the country at Nohant.[1] There he was at his most relaxed and worked with such genuine pleasure that he returned to Paris every year with several new compositions. Yet every winter brought an increase in his suffering so that physical movement became difficult, and then almost impossible, for him. From 1846 to 1847 he hardly walked at all and could not climb a flight of stairs without bouts of painful choking. From that time onwards, he survived only through continual care and treatment.

Around the spring of 1847 his health, worsening daily, developed into an illness from which he was not expected to recover. Although he was saved for the last time, his life was marked by such heartbreak during this period, stemming from the breakdown of his relationship with Mme Sand, that he declared his condition terminal. As Mme de Staël,[2] with her passionate and kindly heart, her fine and lively intellect, said when her feelings overcame her pedantry and reserve: 'in love, there are only beginnings', a declaration founded on her own bitter experience that the heart could not fulfil all the beautiful dreams of the imagination. Ah! If we did not have some blessed examples of human devotion to contradict Mme de Staël, we would respond to all affection with disbelief and scorn, regarding everyone as a *canephor*, that figure in classical allegory who carries flowers in procession to adorn a sacrificial victim.

Chopin at this time often spoke of Mme Sand almost fondly and certainly without bitterness or recrimination. His eyes filled with tears when he uttered her name and, with a kind of passionate gentleness, he gave himself up to the remembered ardour of their once radiant days together. Despite the ploys that friends used to try to deflect his thoughts from this subject and the dreadful upset it caused, it almost seemed as if he wished to destroy himself by suffocating in its lethal vapour. He inhaled the poison eagerly, his final pleasure being

Chapter 8

to witness the final collapse of his final hopes. All attempts to distract his thoughts were in vain since he always returned to the same subject, and even when he spoke of it no more it clearly remained in his thoughts.

However limited the number of days that his physical deterioration left to him, he should have been spared his final painful suffering. With his tender and ardent soul, demanding in its likes and dislikes, he was happy to live among the glorious ghosts that he summoned, and the refined sorrows that he sheltered in his heart. He was yet another victim, a noble and illustrious victim, of the transitory attachments that occur between two contrasting people who suddenly and surprisingly become involved and who, assuming that their feelings will last, build hopes on unrealistic promises and dreams. When the dream is over it is always the one who is the most impressionable, the one most absolute in hopes and affections, who is shattered and wasted. The most exquisite human instincts exercise the most terrible power! They can leave in their wake fire and devastation, like the chargers of the sun which, when the hand of Phaethon lets them wander at will, disrupt the equilibrium of the heavens.[3] Chopin well knew, and often repeated, that when this bond, this long relationship with Mme Sand, was broken, his life was broken too.

During that phase of his illness Chopin's life was despaired of for several days. It was then that M. Gutmann, his most distinguished pupil and, during the last years, his most intimate friend, lavished upon him the most devoted care.[4] Gutmann's attentiveness was such that often when the Princess Czartoryska arrived, visiting him daily fearing that she would never again find him alive, Chopin would ask her with the timidity of the ill, and with his own distinctive delicacy: 'Is Gutmann very tired?' and 'Will he be able to watch over me for longer?'. Chopin's convalescence thereafter was very slow and painful and left him with no more than the merest breath of life, and his appearance changed so much that he was hardly recognisable. Even so, the following summer [1847] brought Chopin the deceptive improvement that seasonal loveliness sometimes grants to the dying, despite the fact that he deprived himself of pure, invigorating country air by refusing to leave Paris.

Although the winter of 1847–48 was filled with a painful sequence of remissions and relapses, he resolved that he would revive his old project of visiting London in the spring. When revolution broke out in February, he was still confined to bed, but with a melancholy effort, he tried to interest himself in the events of the day and spoke of them more than usual. M. Gutmann continued to be his closest intimate and most regular visitor, a care that Chopin gladly accepted until the very end.

By April, Chopin, feeling better, was thinking of visiting that country where he had wanted to go when youth and life still offered him their happiest prospects. However, when the time came for him to leave for England, where his works were generally known and admired and where they had already found an intelligent public, he was in that frame of mind that the English call 'low spirits'.[5] Before his departure, the interest that he had tried to take in the political changes soon disappeared, and he became more taciturn than ever. If, through absent-mindedness, a few words escaped him, they were only utterances of regret. His affection for the small number of people whom he continued to see was tinged with the distress that precedes last farewells. Apathy extended into more and more areas of his life. Art alone retained absolute power over him. For those periods of time (which grew ever shorter), when he could be concerned with it, music absorbed him as completely as it did when he was full of life and hope. Before he left Paris, he gave a concert at the salon of M. Pleyel, one of the friends with whom he had the most frequent, constant and close contact. That same friend who is now rendering homage to the composer's memory and friendship by working zealously to ensure that his grave will have a fitting monument. At this concert, Chopin's public, as exclusive as it was faithful, heard him for the last time.

On his arrival in London, he was welcomed with such warmth and enthusiasm that it helped him to shake off his sadness and dispel his despondency. Perhaps he thought that he would succeed in consigning his depression, and even his past habits, to oblivion. He even neglected his physicians' prescriptions and the precautions that reminded him of his parlous condition. He played in public twice and many times in private concerts, mixed a great deal in society, kept late hours, and risked considerable fatigue without any consideration for his health.[6]

At the home of the Duchess of Sutherland Chopin was presented to the Queen, and the most distinguished salons sought the pleasure of his presence. Then he went to Edinburgh, where the climate proved particularly injurious to him. On his return from Scotland he was so weakened that his physicians wished him to leave England immediately, advice he ignored since he delayed his departure for some time.

Chapter 8

Who could ever know the reason for this delay? He played again at a concert given for Poles – a last expression of love for his country, a last glance, a last sigh and a last expression of regret! It was an occasion where he was lionized, applauded and surrounded by his own people, and he bade them a farewell that they could not know would be forever. What thoughts must have filled his mind as he crossed the sea to return to Paris, a city that had changed so much from the one that he had in 1831 found by chance.

On his return he was greeted with news that was as painful as it was unexpected. Dr Molin, whose advice and resourceful supervision had saved his life in the winter of 1847, and who he believed had kept him alive for some years, was dying.[7] The physician's death was more than a painful loss because it brought on a such morbid despondency, at a crucial time when the mind can exercise so much influence over the course of a disease, that it made him pessimistic that any other doctor could treat him. Henceforth he changed his physicians constantly, becoming dissatisfied with them all. A kind of superstitious depression overwhelmed him so that no bond stronger than life, no love as strong as death, appeared to struggle against his bitter apathy.

From the winter of 1848 onwards Chopin found it impossible to work continuously. Although from time to time he retouched some rough sketches, he was not able to organise his ideas, and a regard for his fame led him to want these sketches to be burned to prevent them being mutilated and otherwise changed into posthumous works unworthy of him.

He left no finished manuscripts, except a last nocturne and a very short waltz as fragments of memory.[8] Last of all, he had planned to write a method for the piano, in which he intended to summarise his ideas upon the theory and technique of his art, the fruit of his long years of hard work, innovation and insightful experience.[9] It was a difficult task and one that demanded intense application even from someone as assiduous as he. By taking refuge in these arid regions did he perhaps wish to avoid the emotions intrinsic to artistic creativity which vary wildly depending whether the heart is serene or troubled? He sought in this work what Byron's Manfred demanded in vain from the powers of magic: *Oblivion!* A forgetting that can be found neither in amusement nor in torpor but in that daily labour which 'allays the storms of the souls' (*der Seele Sturm beschwört*), and in which he doubtless wished to stifle the memories that he could not erase. The poet Schiller, who was also a victim of an inconsolable sadness, likewise sought to soothe his depressing sorrows through work, a strategy that he invoked as a last resort against the bitterness of life at the end of his elegy, 'The Ideal':

> Beschgäftigung, die nie ermattet,
> Die langsam schafft, doch nie zerstört,
> Die zu dem Bau der Ewigkeiten
> Zwar Sandkorn nur für Sandkorn reicht,
> Doch vor der grossen Schuld der Zeiten,
> Minuten, Tage, Jahre streicht.[10]

Yet Chopin could not summon up the strength to realise his plans for the method, the task being too abstract and too tiring. He reflected on the project and spoke of it at different times, but its realisation was beyond him, and he managed only to jot down a few pages that were destroyed with the rest of his sketches.[11]

At last, the illness worsened so visibly that friends began desperately to fear for his life. Soon, he no longer left his bed and hardly spoke. Having been given this news, his sister arrived from Warsaw to be at his bedside where she remained until the end. Throughout he was aware of the anguish, foreboding and increasing sadness all around him, but he gave no outward sign of what he saw; and, although he spoke of his death with a truly Christian calm and resignation, he did not stop making plans for the future. The fondness he always had for changing his address manifested itself again, and he took another apartment and busied himself with organizing the smallest details of its furnishings. Since he had not cancelled the arrangements for moving in, the removal went ahead, so that on the very day of his death his furniture was being carried into the apartment he was never to occupy.

Did he fear that death would not keep its promise and that, having touched him with its finger, it might once again leave him in this world? Did he fear that life would be more cruel if he had to resume living having severed all its ties? Did he experience the contradiction that often affects gifted beings when their fate is in the balance, namely, between the heart that presses on towards the secret of the future, and the mind that dares not glimpse it? Such an opposition can cause the most steadfast spirits to have thoughts that their actions seem to contradict.

From week to week, and soon from day to day, the shadow of death

Chapter 8

loomed ever closer. As the illness entered its last phase, Chopin's suffering became more acute and the crises more frequent, each one bringing the final agony closer. Yet to the end in periods of respite, he regained his presence of mind and strength of will, and throughout lost neither his lucidity of thought nor clarity of purpose. The wishes that he expressed during such intervals attest to the calm solemnity with which he contemplated his approaching demise. He desired to be buried beside Bellini with whom he had frequent and friendly contact during the latter's stay in Paris, and whose grave is in the Père-Lachaise cemetery next to that of Cherubini.[12] His desire to form an acquaintance with the latter (whom he had been brought up to admire) was one of the reasons why, when he left Vienna for London in 1831, he passed through Paris. He now lies between Bellini and Cherubini, two contrasting geniuses to whom he felt himself close to an equal degree, valuing the science of one as much as his instinctive affinity with the other. For Chopin, like the composer of *Norma*, breathed melodic feeling, and, while he aspired to the harmonic depth of the older, more learned man, he wished to unite, in a great and elevated style, the misty vagueness of spontaneous emotion with the prowess of consummate masters.[13]

Maintaining his reserve until the end, Chopin asked to see no one for the last time, but expressed a touching gratitude to all the friends who visited him. The first days of October left neither doubt nor hope. The final moment was drawing near, as the next day, even the next hour, might be his last. His sister and M. Gutmann were constantly with him, and the Countess Delphine Potocka, absent from Paris, returned when she learned of the imminent danger. All those who came to the dying man could not tear themselves away from the sight of this great and beautiful soul at this supreme moment.

However violent or frivolous are the passions that stir the heart, the spectacle of a lingering and beautiful death has an imposing majesty which touches and attracts, softening and elevating even for a soul unprepared for such holy meditation. The slow and gradual departure of one among us for the unknown shores, the mysterious solemnity of his dreams, his recollection of thoughts and actions while still breathing upon that narrow threshold that separates the past from the future, affects us more deeply than anything else in this world. Catastrophes, abysses that gape beneath our feet, conflagrations that engulf whole cities, blood shed in battle, the fate of storm-tossed ships, even the horrors of the plague, none hold our attention like the sight of a soul contemplating the nature of time at the silent door of eternity. Courage and resignation, nobility and emotion in the face of death, by acquainting the soul with its own inevitable dissolution, impress witnesses more profoundly than the most frightful disasters.

There were always some visitors in the salon adjoining Chopin's bedroom, mostly to approach him in turn to receive a gesture or glance, as he was no longer able to speak. On Sunday 15 October, attacks even more painful than before lasted for several hours, and he endured them with patience and great fortitude. The Countess Potocka, who was present, became deeply distressed and wept openly. When Chopin noticed her standing at the foot of his bed – tall, slight, dressed in white, resembling the most beautiful angelic figure imaginable – he supposed her to be a celestial apparition, and during a momentary respite he asked her to sing. Although he was at first thought to be delirious when he eagerly repeated his request, who then dared oppose his wish? The piano having been rolled from the salon to the door of his bedroom, the Countess thereupon began to sing, her voice choking with sobs and with tears streaming down her cheeks. Never before, surely, had this exquisite talent and wonderful voice achieved an expression so full of pathos, and Chopin seemed to suffer less as he listened. She sang that famous *Hymn to the Virgin*, which, it is said, saved the life of Stradella:[14] 'How beautiful it is! My God, how beautiful!', Chopin exclaimed, 'Again – again!' Although overwhelmed with emotion, the Countess had the noble courage to grant this last wish of a friend and compatriot, and again sat at the piano to sing a psalm by Marcello.[15] Suddenly, Chopin felt worse, and everybody became fearful and spontaneously knelt, no one venturing to speak, as the voice of the Countess floated, like a celestial melody, above the sighs and sobs that provided its mournful accompaniment. As night began to fall and the near darkness lent mysterious shadows to the sad scene, Chopin's sister, prostrate near his bed, wept and prayed so long as her beloved brother remained alive.

Although during the night the patient's condition worsened, it improved somewhat on the Monday morning. As if he knew that the end was very near, he requested that the last sacraments should be administered. In the absence of Abbé —, a fellow exile to whom he felt particularly close, he summoned the Abbé Alexandre Jelowicki, one of the most distinguished men among Polish émigrés. When the holy *viaticum* was administered, he received it with deep devotion in the presence of his friends. Shortly after he had them approach

Chapter 8

his bed, one by one, to give each a final blessing, asking that God's grace be upon them and their hopes. Every knee was bent, every head bowed, all eyes were moist with tears, and every heart was heavy yet uplifted.

Still more painful crises continued for the rest of the day. That Monday night and for most of Tuesday, Chopin did not utter a word and seemed no longer able to recognise those around him. Abbé Jelowicki never left him. Only in the evening, about eleven o'clock, did he appear to revive a little, and hardly had he recovered the power of speech than he requested the Abbé to recite with him the prayers and litanies of the dying. This he was able to do in Latin and in an audible and intelligible voice. From then on he leaned his head upon M. Gutmann's shoulder, he who had devoted his days and nights to him during the whole course of the illness.

A convulsive drowsiness lasted into the next day, 17 October 1849, when, at around two o'clock, the final agony commenced. After a short doze, with his brow running with cold sweat he asked in a barely audible voice: 'Who is near me?' He then lowered his head to kiss M. Gutmann's hand, which still supported him, and, while giving this final proof of friendship and gratitude he gave up his soul. Chopin died as he had lived – in loving!

When the doors of the salon were finally opened, his friends surrounded his lifeless corpse, and it was a long time before their tears ceased to flow.

Since Chopin's love for flowers was well known, they were brought in such quantities the next day that the bed on which he lay, and indeed the whole room, disappeared under their many colours. He seemed to rest in a garden, his face having regained a youthfulness, purity and unaccustomed serenity, and his youthful good looks, so long obscured by suffering, reappeared. M. Clésinger immediately sketched his features, their original grace restored by death, in a drawing that was later executed in marble for his tomb.[16]

Chopin's devotion to the genius of Mozart had led him to request that his *Requiem* should be performed at his funeral, and his wish was fulfilled. The funeral ceremonies took place in the Madeleine church on 30 October 1849, having been delayed until this date so that the performance of this great work should be worthy of both master and disciple.[17] The principal artists in Paris were anxious to take part in the service. At the Introit Chopin's own *Funeral March*, orchestrated for the occasion by M. Reber, was heard; while at the Offertory, M.

Lefébure-Wély played Chopin's wonderful *Preludes* in B minor and E minor on the organ.[18] The solo parts of the *Requiem* were sung by Mme Viardot and Mme Castellani; while Lablache, who had sung the Tuba Mirum of this *Requiem* at the burial of Beethoven in 1827, sang it again upon this occasion.[19] M. Meyerbeer, who played the timpani, led the mourners with Prince Adam Czartoryski, while the pallbearers were Prince Alexander Czartoryski, M. Delacroix, M. Franchomme and M. Gutmann.[20]

However inadequate these pages may be to speak of Chopin, we hope that the appeal exerted by his name will make up for what they lack. If we were to add to these lines, imprinted as they are with the memory of his music and all that he held dear, it would be with reflections on how death takes our contemporaries, shattering the bonds first forged by youthful and deluded hearts. In the same year we lost the two dearest friends whom we knew during our years of travel. One of them, Prince Félix Lichnowsky, was killed in action during the civil war! A brave and ill-fated hero, he suffered a frightful death but fell with his burning courage, intrepid calmness and chivalrous daring intact.[21] A young prince of rare intelligence and great energy, his talents had he lived could have been as successfully deployed in political debate and public life as they had been in war. The other friend, Chopin, was slowly devoured by his own flames; his life, lived out of the public gaze, was a thing intangible, revealed only in his music. He ended his days in a foreign land that was never his adoptive country, remaining faithful to an eternal widowhood of his own. He was a poet of the wounded soul, full of secrets, silences and sorrows.

The death of Prince Lichnowsky ended our immediate interest in activities of the groups to which he was linked, while Chopin's death deprived us of the compensations inherent in an all-encompassing friendship. If only this uncompromising artist had lived, his sympathy for our ways of feeling and our approach to art would surely have softened the disappointments and weariness that still lay ahead, just as it strengthened and encouraged our early inclinations and experiments.

Since it is our lot to survive them both, we should like at least to express our sorrow and pay homage upon the grave of the remarkable musician who has just passed from among us. Today, when music is undergoing such a spectacular and wide-ranging transformation, we are reminded of the painters of the fourteenth and fifteenth centuries who, by compressing their miniatures of genius on to the margins of

Chapter 8

parchment, made the first break with the Byzantine style, leaving the most exquisite precedents for the Francias, Peruginos and Raphaels of the future to emulate in their paintings and frescos.[22]

In the past there have been societies with the custom of building memorials to commemorate great men and great deeds, whereby each passer-by was expected to bring a stone to an ever-growing pile: the anonymous endeavour of all. In our era monuments are built in a similar way. However, instead of a crude and shapeless mound, the happy participation of all creates an artwork that is intended not only to commemorate an individual but also to awaken in future ages the feelings that were then experienced by contemporaries. This result is achieved by inviting subscriptions to raise magnificent statues and memorials to those who have added distinction to their nation or epoch.

Immediately after Chopin's death, M. Camille Pleyel conceived a project of this kind: he launched a subscription, which quickly reached a considerable sum, to have a marble monument modelled by M. Clésinger placed in the Père-Lachaise. For our part, in thinking of our long friendship with Chopin and of the admiration we held for him, from his entry into the musical world, we recall that, being an artist like himself, we were the frequent interpreter of his inspirations and, we can boldly say, the interpreter he loved and favoured the most. We, more often than others, received from his own lips insight into the intricacies of his techniques and we, as an interpreter, were identified with his thoughts on his art and with the feelings that he confided to it. We concluded that, under the circumstances, the claims of friendship demanded a more personal testimony of our bitter sorrow and staunch admiration that went beyond merely adding a rough and impersonal stone in homage. It seemed that we should not be true to ourselves if did we not claim the honour of proclaiming our sorrow with a more personal tribute, a privilege permitted to those who can never hope to fill the emptiness in their hearts left by an irreparable loss!

NOTES

CHAPTER 1

1. In the use of 'we' Liszt is surely acknowledging the joint authorship of *Chopin*.
2. The best candidate is probably Jan Vermeer; I am grateful to Professor Colin Platt, author of *Marks of Opulence* (Oxford: Oxford University Press, 2003), for this suggestion.
3. Jakob van Ruysdael (1628–82), Dutch painter famed for dramatic landscapes.
4. Pierre Béranger (1780–1857), French lyric poet noted for setting his verse to popular tunes.
5. Petrarch (1304–74), Italian poet whose epic poem *Africa* was widely regarded as unreadable.
6. Jean de la Fontaine (1621–95), French writer famous for his fables.
7. Mickiewicz, the leader of Polish Romanticism, published his *Balady i romanse* ('Romantic Ballads') in 1822, *Grazyna* (1822), the philosophical poem *Konrad Wallenrod* (1828), and a drama, *Dziady* ('Forefathers' Eve'), in 1832. In most of his writings he sought to inspire the youth of Poland to struggle against foreign oppression.
8. 'Ossian' was purportedly a Gaelic bard whose poetry was collected and published by the Scottish writer and antiquarian James Macpherson (1736–96) as the *Works of Ossian* (1765).
9. The Vale of Tempe, a gorge famous in Antiquity associated with Apollo.
10. Liszt is referring to the *Sonata No. 2* Op. 35; the *Sonata No. 1* Op. 4 did not appear in print until 1851.
11. Jean-Paul (Johann Paul Friedrich Richter) (1763–1825) a German writer whose work was characterised by grotesque humour.

CHAPTER 2

1. Madame de Pompadour (née Jeanne Poisson) (1721–64), mistress of the French king Louis XV.
2. The best candidates for the female role models alluded to are as follows. Lucrezia Borgia (1480–1519) who, as sometime wife of Giovanni Sforza, a scion of the Milanese ducal family, came to epitomise the ruthless politics

Notes

and sexual corruption of court life in Renaissance Italy. Marie de la Grange d'Arquien (1641–1716) wielded considerable political influence as the consort of Jan III Sobieski King of Poland (ruled 1674–96). Isabella d'Este (1474–1539), as the wife of Francesco Gonzaga Duke of Mantua, became a leading cultural and political figure of the Italian Renaissance.

3   Jan III Sobieski King of Poland (1629–96), hero of the wars against the Turks whose army lifted the Ottoman siege of Vienna in 1683. Sobieski wanted to unify Christendom in a crusade to expel the Turks from south eastern Europe including, of course, Liszt's own beloved Hungary.

4   This reference is probably to Bolesław III Krzywousty, 'a predatory warrior' who was invested with Pomerania in 1135. See N. Davies: *God's Playground: A History of Poland* (Oxford: Clarendon, 1981), vol i, p. 72.

5   Paolo Veronese (1528–88), Venetian painter of the Renaissance who specialised in opulent group portraits.

6   The Polish monarchy was, for many centuries, an elective office open to all members of the nobility.

7   *Kontusz*, a long outer robe worn by Polish and Lithuanian nobles.

8   [Liszt's note] In England, the Hungarian costume worn by Prince Nicolas Esterházy at the coronation of George IV and valued at millions of florins, is still remembered.

9   *Zupan* was an inner garment worn with the *kontusz*, originally an expensive item of aristocratic attire. Wearing the *zupan* became widespread in nineteenth century Poland.

10 Pindar, a poet of classical Greece (died c. 440 BC).

11 [Liszt's note] It is well known that many Polish names enrich the martyrology of the Catholic Church. The Papacy granted to the Order of Trinitarians, or the 'Brothers of the Redemption', committed to redeem Christians enslaved by the infidels, the exclusive privilege of wearing a red belt on a white habit in memory of the Order's martyrs. Many of the latter came from establishments close to the frontier such as the one at Kamieniec-Podolski.

12 *Pan Tadeusz* (1834), widely acknowledged as a (Lithuanian) national epic of liberation and revival. One of its many themes is the celebration of the democratic ideals widely held by the Lithuanian and Polish troops who fought as part of Napoleon's doomed army in Russia in 1812. Towards the end of *Pan Tadeusz* Mickiewicz wrote a description of the polonaise, perhaps providing Liszt with a point of departure for much of this chapter. After the fall of communist Poland, the epic was made into a feature-film directed by Andrzej Wajda.

13 Thaddeus Kościuszko (1746–1817) was an officer who distinguished himself during both the American War of Independence (on the colonists' side) and the failed Polish Uprising of 1794.

14 [Liszt's note] One of them, in F major, has remained particularly famous.

Notes

It was published with a vignette showing the composer blowing his brains out with a pistol, a romantic fiction long accepted as fact. [Translator's note] Prince Michał Ogiński (1765–1833) is credited with the evolution of the polonaise into an 'independent work for the salon rather than for court dancing'. Ogiński's involvement in the abortive Polish Uprising of 1794 'only increased the national resonance of his compositions [and] assured the popularity of the polonaise [. . .] across much of Europe'. See S. Sadie (ed.), *New Grove Dictionary* entry on the 'Polonaise' (vol. xx, pp. 45–7, S. Downes).

15   The 'Bard of Erin' refers to the Irish poet Thomas Moore (1779–1852) who secured an international reputation for his collections of *Irish Melodies* (1808–34).

16   Karol Józef Lipiński (1790–1861); Polish violinist who composed several *rondos alla polacca* as part of his prolific output of dance music. He dedicated an *Allegro de Concert* to Liszt. See S. Sadie (ed.), *New Grove Dictionary* entry on Lipinski (vol. xiv. pp. 734–5, J. Powroźniak / Z. Chechlińska).

17   Joseph Mayseder (1789–1863), Austrian violinist and composer.

18   Carl Maria von Weber (1786–1826) wrote two polonaises for piano: *Grande Polonaise* Op. 21 (1808) and *Polacca Brillante (L'hilarité)* Op. 72 (1819). Why Liszt should have formed a high opinion of the latter is puzzling since it is a work that treats the dance in the Italian manner.

19   [Liszt's note] Among the treasures of Prince Radziwitt at Nieswirz were to be seen, in the days of former splendour, twelve sets of horse trappings, each of a different colour and encrusted with precious stones. Also to be seen there were the twelve life-size apostles in massive silver. This luxury is not astonishing when we consider that the family – descended from the last Grand Pontiff of Lithuania, to whom, when he embraced Christianity was given lands which had been consecrated to the worship of heathen deities – still possessed eight hundred thousand serfs towards the end of the last century. Among the treasure was a curious relic that is still in existence; a picture of St John the Baptist, bearing the inscription: 'In the name of the Lord, John, thou shalt be Conqueror.' It was found by Jean Sobieski after his victory under the walls of Vienna in the tent of the Vizier Kara Mustapha and presented after the king's death by Marie d'Arquin to a Prince Radziwiłł with an inscription in her own handwriting indicating its origin and her presentation of it. The autograph, with the royal seal, is on the reverse of the canvas.

20   *Polonaise* Op. 40 No. 1 (1840). Weber's work is the *Polacca Brillante* referred to in note 18 above.

21   *Polonaise* Op. 44 (1841).

22   Liszt quotes freely from the opening stanza of Byron's poem, *The Dream*, lines 5–11: 'And dreams in their development have breath, / And tears, and tortures, and the touch of joy; / They leave a weight upon our waking

Notes

thoughts, / They take a weight from off waking toils, / They do divide our being; they become / A portion of ourselves as of our time, / And look like heralds of eternity'.

23 *Polonaise-Fantasie* Op. 61.

CHAPTER 3

1 Artemis was the 'divine huntress' of mythology.
2 The tale of the runner, the athlete, huntress and reluctant bride Atalanta and her match, Hippomenes, is told by the Roman poet Ovid (43 BC– c. AD 18) in his *Metamorphoses* (Book 10).
3 *Houri*, a nymph of the Muslim paradise, here applied allusively to a voluptuous woman (*OED*).
4 Balzac's dedication of his novel *Modeste Mignon* (1844) to his Polish mistress (and future wife) the Countess Eveline Hanska.
5 Byron's history play *The Two Foscari* (1821) was later adapted as a libretto for Verdi's opera *I due Foscari*.
6 'Attic spirit' here refers to an attachment to the refined elegance that characterised classical Athens.
7 [Liszt's note] The custom of drinking the health of woman from her own shoe to be especially honoured is one of the most original traditions of Polish gallantry. [Translator's note] The following awkward and digressive sentence has been cut from the text here. 'They alone fulfil the impassioned dreams of poets like M. de Chateaubriand who, in the feverish sleeplessness of youth, created a female demon and charmer only to find a single resemblance in a Polish girl of sixteen: "an Eve, innocent yet fallen; ignorant of all yet knowing all; virgin yet lover, part-odalisque part-Valkyrie; a feminine fusion of age and beauty, a classical sylph made flesh, a new Flora". A being that, freed from the yoke of the seasons, M. de Chateaubriand was afraid to meet again!' Liszt notes that he took his quotations from Chateaubriand's *Memoires d'outre-tombe* ('Memoirs from beyond the grave') (1849–50), vol. i, *Incantation*, and from *Atala* vol. iii.

CHAPTER 4

1 An urn for collecting tears of sorrow.
2 Dryads were tree nymphs (nature deities) often linked to the goddess Artemis, Oreads were nymphs of mountain forests and glens, and Oceanides were sea nymphs.
3 Charles Nodier (1780–1844), French poet and novelist whose *La Fée aux miettes* (1832) and *Trilby, ou le lutin d'Argail* (1824) both drew on folkloric and 'fairy' subject matter.

Notes

4 Areopagus, the Hill of Ares in classical Athens that gave its name to a tribunal that met there.
5 The Dorians were a people who dominated much of Greece in the centuries after 1100 BC.
6 [Liszt's note] In its polite forms of address, Polish is strongly marked by the hyperbole of oriental speech. The titles 'most powerful' and 'most enlightened lord' are still the norm. 'Benefactor' (*dobrodzji*) is used in normal conversation, while the common greeting between men, or between a man and a woman is 'I fall at your feet' (*padam do nog*). The normal greeting between people has an ancient solemnity and simplicity: 'Glory to God' (*Slawa Bohu*).
7 [Liszt's note] Heine: *Salon*, 'Chopin'. [Translator's note] See H. Heine / C. G. Leland [Hans Breitman] (tr.): *The Salon, or Letters on Art, Music, Popular Life and Politics*, 'Tenth Letter: the French Stage' (1837, Heinemann, 1893) pp. 279–80 for the quoted extracts in this paragraph.
8 The story of Captain van der Decken, the 'Flying Dutchman' condemned to sail his ship forever, is one of the great legends of the sea. Liszt is referring to Heine's treatment of the story in his satirical novel *Aus den Memoiren des Herrn von Schnalbelewopski* ('Memoirs of Mr von Schnalbelewopski') (1833).
9 The novel *Undine* (1811) by F. H. K. La Motte Fouqué (1777–1843) based on the Teutonic folk tale of a female water sprite became one of the best-loved children's stories of the century.
10 A pre-sunrise triangle of light, known as the 'false dawn', made up of interplanetary dust particles.
11 A giant star in Taurus (near Orion).
12 In the New Testament, Herodias is the mother of Salome and the wife of King Herod. In Heine's poem *Atta Troll* (1841), a mock-picaresque satire on Romanticism, Herodias appears on horseback as a 'wandering spook'. See H. Heine / Scheffauer (tr.): *Atta Troll* (Sidgwick & Jackson, 1913), Canto XIX, st. 21–34 and Canto XX st. 18–31.
13 Giacomo Meyerbeer (1791–1864), German opera composer based in Paris in the 1830s and 1840s, achieved European fame with three works in particular: *Robert le diable* (1831), *Les Huguenots* (1836) and *La Prophète* (1849).
14 Adolphe Nourrit (1802–39), a tenor at the Paris Opera and much admired by Chopin; he committed suicide in 1839.
15 Ferdinand Hiller (1811–85), German composer and conductor based in Paris until 1835, close friend of Chopin and dedicatee of his *Nocturnes* Op 15.
16 Arachne was a mortal who challenged the goddess Athena to a weaving contest. Having presumed to depict the promiscuity of the gods in her weave, Arachne was turned into a spider.

Notes

17 Julian Niemcewicz (1758–1841), Polish poet, playwright, revolutionary and statesman published his *Historical Songs* ('Śpiewy historyczne') in 1816. There is no evidence that Chopin set any of them.
18 In this context it should be noted that Chopin and Mickiewicz 'were never particularly close'. Samson: *Chopin*, p. 134.
19 The 'suicide lover' referred to is Gustaw from *Dziady* ('Forefathers' Eve'), who kills himself when the love of his life leaves him to marry a rich duke.
20 The poet referred to here is probably Petrarch (1304–74), whose work was close to Liszt's heart, and who stressed the compatibility of human creativity with deep religious faith.

CHAPTER 5

1 Liszt took this phrase from the title of Goethe's autobiography: *Aus meinem Leben: Dichtung und Wahrheit* ('From my Life: Poetry and Truth') (1811–31).
2 Liszt had first suggested that *'génie oblige'*, the idea that genius imposed its own obligations, should become the guiding principle for any 'artist of the future' in an obituary tribute to Paganini (*La Revue et gazette musicale*, 23 August 1840). See Walker: *Liszt: Virtuoso Years*, pp. 176–7.
3 Torquato Tasso (1544–95), the Italian poet and courtier famous for his epic poem *La Gerusalemme liberata* (1574), was embraced by the Romantic generation for his personal sufferings and persecuted genius. The quotation is from *La Gerusalemme liberata*, Book II, stanza 16.
4 The following was excised from the text: 'Although ordinary folk have a certain respect for painful feelings, which exert the attraction of the unknown and arouse a kind of admiration, they appreciate them only at a distance, and flee them to boring tranquillity, being just as likely to swoon at their description as to turn away from them'.
5 The upheaval referred to here is the 'July Revolution' in Paris (1830).
6 Horace (65–8 BC), Roman poet noted for his urbanity and tolerance.
7 Liszt here probably wanted to refer to Paul, fifth Duc de Noailles (1739–1824), a chemist and member of the Academy of Sciences.
8 In Greek mythology, Procrustes was a brigand who ensnared travellers with hospitality only to bind them to a bed that they were made to fit by amputation.
9 [Liszt's note] Polish cannot be reproached for lacking in harmony or musical appeal. The frequency of the consonants is not always responsible for the harshness of a language but rather the way they combine. Indeed it might be said that some are dull and cold because they lack strongly marked sounds. The frequent repetition of certain consonants gives shade, rhythm and vigour to the language, the preponderance of

Notes

vowels creating a kind of clear pale quality that must be relieved by darker shades. The sharp, rough clashing of heterogeneous consonants painfully injures the ear. Slav languages, it is true, use many consonants but generally in combinations that are sonorous and pleasant to the ear, and the quality of the sounds is rich, full and varied. They are not compressed but extend over a considerable range and have a variety of intonations. There is nothing dry in the sound of the letter Ł, although it is almost impossible to pronounce if not learned in childhood; it is like the touch of thick woollen velvet, rough but supple. In Polish there are many words that imitate the sound of the object designated. The frequent repetitions of *ch* (*h* aspirated), of *sz* (*ch* in French), of *rz*, of *cz*, so frightening to the eye, have, however, nothing barbaric in their sounds, being pronounced (like the French) *geai*, *tche*, and generally facilitate the meanings through sound. The word *dzwięk* (read *dzwïinque*) meaning 'sound' offers a characteristic example; it would be difficult to find a word that can reproduce so well the resonance of a tuning fork on the ear. Among the consonants accumulated in groups that produce greatly varied sounds – metallic, buzzing, hissing, growling – there are a number of mingled diphthongs and vowels that become slightly nasal; for example, the *a* and the *e* being sounded as *on* and *in* (in French), when they are accompanied by a cedilla. Alongside the *c* (*tse* in French), pronounced with great softness, sometimes *ć* (*tsie* in French), the accented *s* is almost chirped. The *z* has three sounds: the *ż* (*jais*), the *z* (*zed*) and the *z* (*zied* all in French). The *y* is a muffled vowel that, like the Ł, cannot be sounded in French, and which like it, gives a glow to the language. These fine and delicate features give Polish women a lingering and singing accent, which they carry over into other tongues, and which they employ in both sad and serious conversations with a curious enunciation and a sort of childish lisp. They mingle slivery laughter and cries of interruption with a musical lingering upon higher notes, from which they quickly descend by chromatic tones to rest upon a low note. Then they go into countless abrupt and original modulations that disorient the ear unaccustomed to such lovely warbling, to which they give a deceptive air of irony and mockery peculiar to the song of certain birds. They love to twitter, and piquant intervals, unexpected pauses and charming nuances appear naturally in their chatter, making Polish much sweeter and caressing than when spoken by men. The latter elegantly give it a masculine sonority, which is peculiarly adapted to the tradition of eloquence once so cultivated in Poland. Poetry finds in these rich and varied materials, a diversity of rhythms, prosody, rhymes and an abundance of assonance that enables the language musically to follow the feelings and scenes that it depicts. The analogy between Polish and Russian has been rightly compared to that between Latin and Italian. The Russian language is more mellifluous, lingering, and more yearning

Notes

than Polish, its cadences being peculiarly fitted for song. Its finest poetry, such as that of Zukowski and Pushkin, seems to contain a melody already present in the metre; for example, certain stanzas (from *Le Châle noir*, or the *Talisman*) seem poised to flow into an *arioso* or a sweet *cantabile*. Ancient Slavonic, the language of the Eastern Church, possesses great majesty; more guttural than the idioms that have flowed from it, it has a severe and measured grandeur like the Byzantine paintings that adorn its rites. Its characteristics are those of a sacred language that has been used only for the expression of one feeling and which remains unaltered by the demands of the secular world. [Translator's Note] The Russian writer, Alexander Pushkin (1799–1837), a political and literary radical, based his short poem 'The Talisman' on a Muslim sorceress and her secret power. 'Le Châle noir' ('The Black Shawl') by Alexis de Valon (1850) probably refers to a translation by the Russian poet and patriot Vasily Andrevich Zhukovsky (1783–1852).

CHAPTER 6

1 Angelica Catalani (1780–1849), a renowned Italian soprano who met Chopin as a child in Warsaw.
2 Liszt gets his facts wrong here; Chopin started his lessons with Adalbert Żywny (1756–1842), a Bohemian composer, when he was six. Samson: *Chopin*, p. 11.
3 Prince Antoni Henryk Radziwiłł (1775–1833) was a cellist and composer whose *Faust* was published posthumously in 1835. The Chopin family later expressed its dismay at Liszt's assertion that Radziwiłł had subsidised Chopin's education.
4 The following italicised passages are quoted from George Sand's novel *Lucrezia Floriani* (1846) and are here translated from Liszt's published text. The page references in the following notes are from Sand's definitive edition of the novel republished in G. Sand: *Lucrezia Floriani* (1846, Paris: Michel Levy Frères 1867). For a recent English-language edition of the novel, see G. Sand / J. Eker (tr.): *Lucrezia Floriani* (Chicago: Academy Chicago Publishers, 1993).
5 G. Sand: *Lucrezia Floriani* (1846, Paris: Michel Levy Frères 1867), p. 4.
6 Ibid., p. 4.
7 Ibid., p. 4.
8 Ibid., p. 50.
9 Ibid., p. 4.
10 Ibid., p. 5.
11 Ibid., p. 5.
12 Ibid., p. 5.
13 Ibid., pp. 5–6.

Notes

14 Bernardino Luini (c. 1480–1532) was an Italian painter whose reworking of Leonardo's style made him fashionable in the first half of the nineteenth century.
15 Liszt's visit to the Chopin family must have taken place during his tour of Poland in the spring of 1843.
16 For confirmation of Chopin's connection with the Czetwertyński family see Goldberg: *Chopin's Warsaw*, p. 157.
17 For Chopin's association with the Zamoyski and Radziwiłł families, see ibid., p. 157, and with the Jabłonowskis, ibid., pp. 183–4.
18 The *Dictamus fraxinella* [Burning bush] has been used by gardeners since the eighteenth century for its pervasive fragrance of lemon, almonds and vanilla.
19 Cracovienne, Krakowiak in Polish, is a dance from the Kraków district in 2/4 time with distinctive syncopation.
20 Sand: *Lucrezia Floriani* p. 43.
21 Johann Nepomuk Hummel (1778–1837), Austrian composer, pianist and teacher, may be regarded as a transitional figure between the Viennese classical style and the new Romanticism. He served as Kappellmeister to the grand-ducal court at Weimar from 1820 until his death.
22 Countess Delfina Potocka (1807–77), famous for her salon and for her singing voice, became a close friend of the composer. As already noted, Chopin was close to the politically conservative group of exiles around Prince Adam Czartoryski.
23 Julian Fontana (1810–69), pianist and composer, and one of Chopin's closest friends from his Warsaw days, acted as the composer's factotum during the 1830s. Jan Ostrowski (1782–1845), a politician and soldier, was sometime commander of the National Guard during the 1830–31 uprising, while General Count Szembek (dates unknown) was a divisional commander during the defence of Warsaw in the early weeks of the revolution.

CHAPTER 7

1 *Indiana*, *Valentine* and *Jacques* all appeared in 1832–34. *Lélia* (1833), part novel and part poem, part allegory and part work of realism, is the tale of a woman's futile quest for love and sexual fulfilment, and provoked a literary storm when it was published. The quotation is from 'Letter Four: To Rollinat' in G. Sand / S. Rabinovitch and P. Thomson (tr.): *Lettres d'un voyageur* (Paris, 1834–35; Penguin, 1987) pp. 131–3. Sand's *Lettres*, an emotionally charged travelogue of a young man in Italy, first appeared in *La Revue des deux mondes* in 1834–35.
2 Pygmalion was the King of Cyprus who fell in love with the ivory statue of a beautiful woman; thanks to the intercession of the goddess Aphrodite the statue came alive and married him.

Notes

3 Galatea in Greek mythology is a 'milk-white' maiden whose living, breathing beauty cannot be concealed.
4 Sand's heroine is compared to three of the most transgressive of Byron's eponymous heroes: the Turkish pirate in the poem *Lara* (1814), with his secret homosexuality; the murderous brother in *Cain* (1821); and the Faustian count in *Manfred* (1817).
5 The Amazons were a race of ferocious women-warriors encountered by Jason and his Argonauts on their quest for the Golden Fleece.
6 Medusa, the mythological Gorgon decapitated by the Greek hero Perseus, had a gaze so powerful that it could turn mortals to stone.
7 The reference is to the last lines of Goethe's *Faust*, 'das Ewigweibliche zieht uns hinan' ('the eternal feminine draws us aloft'), which affirm the power of salvation through the feminine.
8 [Translator's note] Some highly discursive and obtuse material on *Lélia* (amounting to some ninety words) paragraph has been excised from this to improve sense. The sentence-order has also been slightly modified.
9 Byron's *The Lament of Tasso* (1817), a poem inspired by the incarceration of the creative spirit.
10 The 'last war' refers to the Polish Uprising of 1830–31.
11 Peri is a benign spirit that features in Thomas Moore's *Lalla Rookh: An Oriental Romance* (1817). In the Romantic imagination, she came to symbolise an ideal of womanhood, of female tenderness, selflessness, grace and beauty that was capable of redeeming both itself and others.
12 Thus, according to Liszt, did Chopin become one of Sand's creative projects.
13 Sand loved Nature and advocated close study of the natural world as an antidote to romantic introspection and intellectual self-analysis.
14 Geneviève is a working-class victim in Sand's novel *André* (1834).
15 [Liszt's note] *Lettres d'un voyageur*.
16 Liszt notes that the quote is taken from Sand's novel *Spiridion* (1839). The imaginary world alluded to is that of E. T. A. Hoffmann (1776–1822), a leading light in German Romantic literature.
17 [Liszt's note] *Lettres d'un voyageur*.
18 Sand: *Lucrezia Floriani*, p. 36. With *Waverley* (1814) Sir Walter Scott (1771–1832) pioneered the genre of the historical novel.
19 The 'Sibyl', or prophetess, was an important figure in Roman myth and history. There were several sibyls in the ancient world, all of them associated with important temple-oracle sites.
20 Chopin journeyed South in the winter of 1838–39.
21 Mignon was the doomed young singer in Goethe's *Wilhelm Meister* (1821).
22 [Liszt's note] *Lucrezia Floriani*. Quote not found in the 1867 edition.
23 Ibid. Quote not found in the 1867 edition.

Notes

24 Sand: *Lucrezia Floriani*, p. 36.
25 Carolus Linnaeus (1707–78), Swedish botanist, invented the notion of a 'petal time clock' from which one could tell the time of day by watching flowers open.
26 Liszt is referring to Sand's account of her visit to Majorca with Chopin, *Un Hiver à Majorque* (1842).
27 Greek fire (or 'sea fire'), a weapon-system deployed by the Byzantines, was a kind of medieval flame-thrower that fired an incendiary mixture that burned intensely in water.

CHAPTER 8

1 Nohant refers to George Sand's *petit chateau* near the village of La Châtre in the Berry region.
2 Germaine [Baronne] de Staël (1766–1817), one of the most influential writers of the early Romantic movement, is perhaps best remembered for her novel *Corinne* (1807).
3 Phaethon, son of Helios (god of the Sun), was killed by Zeus for driving his chariot erratically across the heavens.
4 Adolphe Gutmann (1819–82), German pianist and composer, was Chopin's favourite pupil and dedicatee of the *Scherzo* Op. 39.
5 [Liszt's note] Chopin's works had been widely known and appreciated in England for several years, having frequently been performed by the best virtuosi. We find in a pamphlet published in London by Wessel and Stapleton, entitled 'An Essay on the Works of F. Chopin', some appropriate lines prefaced by a couplet from Shelley (from *Peter Bell the Third*) that could fittingly be applied to Chopin: 'He was a mighty poet – and / A subtle-soul'd psychologist'. The author of this pamphlet writes with enthusiasm of that 'originative genius untrammelld by conventionalities, unfettered by pedantry'; and of those 'outpourings of an unwordly and tristful soul – those musical floods of tears, and gushes of pure joyfulness, – those exquisite embodiments of beautiful thoughts, – those infinitesmal delicacies' that give value even to Chopin's slightest sketches. Later, the English writer goes on to say that: 'One thing is certain, to play Chopin's *Préludes* and *Studies* is to be neither more nor less than a finished pianist, and moreover, to comprehend them thoroughly, to give a life and a tongue to their infinite and most eloquent subtleties of expression, involves the necessity of being in no less a degree a poet than a pianist, a thinker than a musician. Commonplace is instinctively avoided in all the works of Chopin; a stale cadence or a trite progression; a hum-drum subject or a hackneyed sequence; a vulgar twist of the melody or a worn-out passage; a meagre harmony or an unskilful counterpoint, may in vain be looked for throughout the entire range of

Notes

his compositions, the prevailing characteristics of which are a feeling, as uncommon as beautiful, a treatment as original as felicitous, a melody and a harmony, as new, fresh, vigorous, and striking as they are utterly unexpected, and out of the ordinary track. In taking up one of Chopin's works, you are entering, as it were, a fairy land, untrodden by human footsteps, a path, hitherto unfrequented, but by the great composer himself; and a faith, and a devotion, *a desire to appreciate, and a determination to understand*, are absolutely necessary, to do it anything like adequate justice [. . .]. Chopin in his *Polonaises* and in his *Mazoures* has aimed at those characteristics, which distinguish the national music of his country so markedly from that of all others, that quaint idiosyncrasy, that identical wildness and fantasticality, that delicious mingling of the sad and the cheerful, which invariably and forcibly individualize the music of those northern countries, whose language delights, in combination of consonants [. . .]'. '[Translator's note] This quotation is taken verbatim, in English, from the first edition. The 'essay' was written by James William Davison (1813–85) music critic, editor of the *Musical World* (1843–85) and critic at the London *Times* (1846–78).

6 For details of Chopin's engagements in Britain see Samson: *Chopin* pp. 254–8.

7 Dr. Jean-Jacques Molin, a homeopathic doctor, achieved some success in treating Chopin's consumption.

8 Chopin in fact left a considerable number of unpublished works at his death; see Samson: *Chopin*, pp. 303–4, for a list of his posthumously published music.

9 For a discussion of *Le projet de méthode*, see Samson: *Chopin*, pp. 86–7.

10 [Liszt's note]: Schiller, *L'Idéal*. Liszt quotes the last stanza of Schiller's poem 'To the Ideal': And thou, so pleased, with her uniting, / To charm the soul-storm into peace, / Sweet toil, in toil itself delighting, / That more it laboured, less could cease, / Though but by grains thou aidest the pile / The vast eternity uprears, / At least thou strikest from time the while / Life's debt, the minutes, days and years'. F. Schiller / E. Bulwer-Lytton (tr.): *Poems and Ballads of Schiller* (Leipzig: Tauchnitz, 1844), pp. 71–3.

11 The *Méthode* was not destroyed at Chopin's death: see Samson: *Chopin*, p. 282.

12 Vicenzo Bellini (1801–35), Italian opera composer and protégé of Rossini, spent the last two years of his life in Paris and became acquainted with Chopin. Maria Luigi Cherubini (1760–1842), Italian composer and Director of the Paris Conservatoire (after 1822).

13 *Norma*, Bellini's greatest success, was premièred in 1831.

14 Alessandro Stradella (c. 1645–82), Italian composer whose fame rested on his church music.

Notes

15 Benedetto Marcello (1686–1739), Venetian composer and poet, who gained eminence for his settings of psalms.
16 Jean Baptiste Auguste Clésinger (1814–83), a sculptor, had married George Sand's daughter, Solange, after a whirlwind affair in 1847. The monument he sculpted still marks the composer's grave.
17 The Madeleine, completed in 1840, was regarded as the venue of choice for 'society' funerals.
18 Henri Reber (1807–80), French composer, teacher and sometime professor of harmony and (later) of composition at the Paris Conservatoire. Louis Lefébure-Wély (1817–69), French composer and Organist at the Madeleine.
19 Pauline Viardot (1821–1910), French singer and composer, was famous for her roles in operas by Gluck, Rossini, Meyerbeer and Berlioz. Luigi Lablache (1794–1858), Italian bass, was famed for his roles in operas by Rossini, Bellini and Donizetti.
20 August Franchhomme (1808–84), French cellist, was a close friend of Chopin and dedicatee of the *Cello Sonata* in G minor Op. 65; Prince Alexander Czartoryski, brother of Prince Adam, was married to Marcellina Czartoryska. Eisler: *Chopin's Funeral*, p. 146.
21 Prince Félix Lichnowsky (1814–48), German nobleman of liberal political views, was close to Liszt during the 1840s. He was hacked to death by a Frankfurt mob during the revolutionary violence of 1848.
22 Francia [Francesco Raibolini] (c. 1450–1520), Bolognese artist and engraver, gained a new celebrity in the nineteenth century for Catholic pietism in a conservative style. Perugino [Pietro Vannucci] (1450–1517), Italian painter, worked on frescos in the Sistine Chapel, Rome. Raphael [Raffaello Sanzio] (1483–1520), one of the most renowned painters of the Italian Renaissance.

SELECT BIBLIOGRAPHY

Place of publication London unless otherwise entered

Anderson, B.: *Imagined Communities: Reflections on the Origin and Spread of Nationalism* (Verso, rev. second edition, 2006).
Atwood, W. G.: *Fryderyk Chopin: Pianist from Warsaw* (New York: Columbia University Press, 1987).
——: *The Parisian Worlds of Frédéric Chopin* (New Haven: Yale University Press, 1999).
Broers, M.: *Europe after Napoleon: Revolution, Reaction and Romanticism, 1815–48* (Manchester: Manchester University Press, 1996).
Chopin, F. / Opieński H. / Voynich E. L. (ed./tr.): *Chopin's Letters* (New York: Dover, 1988).
Davies, N.: *God's Playground: A History of Poland* (Oxford: Clarendon Press, 1981). 2 vols.
Deák I.: *Lawful Revolution: Louis Kossuth and the Hungarians, 1848–1849* (New York: Columbia University Press, 1979).
Eisler, B.: *Chopin's Funeral* (Abacus, 2004).
Gibbs, C. H. / Gooley, D. (eds): *Franz Liszt and His World* (Princeton and Oxford: Princeton University Press, 2006).
Gildea, R.: *Barricades and Borders: Europe 1800–1914* (Oxford: Oxford University Press, 2003).
Goldberg, H. (ed.): *The Age of Chopin: Interdisciplinary Inquiries* (Bloomington: Indiana University Press, 2004).
Gooley, D.: *The Virtuoso Liszt* (Cambridge: Cambridge University Press, 2004).
Hamilton, K. (ed.): *The Cambridge Companion to Liszt* (Cambridge: Cambridge University Press, 2005).
Jack, B.: *George Sand: A Woman's Life Writ Large* (Vintage, 2001).
Jedlicki, J.: *A Suburb of Europe: Nineteenth Century Polish Approaches to Western Civilization* (Budapest: Central Europe University Press, 1999).
Lenneberg, H.: *Witnesses and Scholars: Studies in Musical Biography* (Gordon and Breach 1988).
Liszt, F.: *F. Chopin* (Paris: Escudier, 1852).
—— / Broadhouse, J. (tr.): *The Life of Chopin* (Reeves, 1899 and 1912).

Select Bibliography

—— / Cook, M. W. (tr.): *Life of Chopin* (Boston: Ditson 1863, London: Reeves, 1877).
—— / Waters, E. N. (tr.): *Frédéric Chopin by Franz Liszt* (Free Press of Glencoe, Collier-Macmillan 1963).
—— / Chantavoine, J. (ed.): *Pages romantiques* (Paris: Alcan, 1912).
—— / Suttoni C. (ed./tr.): *An Artist's Journey: lettres d'un bachelier ès musique, 1835–41* (Chicago: University of Chicago Press, 1989).
—— / Williams, A. (ed./tr.): *Franz Liszt: Selected Letters* (Oxford: Clarendon Press, 1998).
Niecks, F.: *Frederick Chopin: As a Man and Musician* (Novello, 1888), 2 vols.
Pekacz, J. T. (ed.): *Musical Biography: Towards New Paradigms* (Aldershot: Ashgate, 2006).
Sadie, S. (ed.): *The New Grove Dictionary of Music and Musicians* (Macmillan, second edition, 2001).
Saffle, M. and Deaville, J. (eds): *New Light on Liszt and His Music: Essays in Honour of Alan Walker's 65th Birthday* (Stuyvesant: Pendragon, 1997).
Samson, J. (ed.): *The Cambridge Companion to Chopin* (Cambridge: Cambridge University Press, 1992).
—— (ed.): *The Cambridge History of Nineteenth Century Music* (Cambridge: Cambridge University Press, 2002).
——: *Chopin* (Oxford: Oxford University Press, 1996, Master Musicians series, S. Sadie (ed.)).
—— (ed.): *Chopin Studies* (Cambridge: Cambridge University Press, 1988).
—— / Rink, J. (eds.): *Chopin Studies 2* (Cambridge: Cambridge University Press, 1994).
Sand, G. / Eker, J. (tr.): *Lucrezia Floriani* (Paris 1846, Chicago: Academy Chicago Publishers, 1993).
Todd, R. Larry (ed.): *Nineteenth-Century Piano Music* (Routledge, second edition, 2004).
Walicki, A.: *Philosophy and Romantic Nationalism: The Case of Poland* (Notre Dame: University of Notre Dame Press 1994).
Walker, A.: *Franz Liszt, Volume One: The Virtuoso Years, 1811–47* (Faber and Faber, revised edition 1988).
——: *Franz Liszt, Volume Two: The Weimar Years, 1848–61* (Ithaca: Cornell University Press 1989).
——: *Franz Liszt, Volume Three: The Final Years, 1861–86* (Ithaca: Cornell University Press, 1996).
White, H. / Murphy, M. (eds): *Musical Constructions of Nationalism: Essays on the History and Ideology of European Musical Culture 1800–1945* (Cork: Cork University Press, 2001).
Wolff, L.: *Inventing Eastern Europe: The Map of Civilization on the Mind of the Enlightenment* (Stanford: Stanford University Press, 1994).

INDEX

Agoult, [Comtesse] Marie d' 6, 11, 42n.23, 43n.26
Alexander the Great, [King] 23
Anderson, Benedict 14–15
Ariès, Philippe 30–1

Bach, Johann Sebastian 37–8
Balzac, Honoré de 6, 19–20, 34, 81, 141n.4
   Béatrix 6
   Cousin Bette 19–20
Batthyány, Lajos 7, 12, 16, 26
Beethoven, Ludwig van 3, 38–9, 114–15, 136
Bellini, Vincenzo 133, 149n.12
   Norma 133
Bennett, Joseph 36
Béranger, Pierre 61
Berlioz, Hector 1, 3, 8, 26, 39, 84, 103
   Benvenuto Cellini 39
   Symphonie Fantastique 3
Boleslaw III, [Prince] 67
Boswell, James 37
   Life of Samuel Johnson 37
Breitkopf und Härtel [Publishers] 12–13, 33
Byron, [Baron] George 26, 31, 74–5, 82, 120, 131
   'A Dream' 31, 47n.94, 75
   The Lament of Tasso 120, 147n.9
   Manfred 122, 131, 147n.4
   The Two Foscari 82

Carl Alexander, [Grand Duke] 23–4
Catalani, Angelica 107
Charles X, [King] 42n.17
Cherubini, Maria Luigi 133
Chopin, Frédéric
   Ballade No.2 Op.38 9
   Études Op.10 5
   Études Op.25 6
   Nocturnes Op.9 42n.22
   Piano Concerto No. 2 63, 117
   Polonaise Op.40/1 74
   Polonaise Op.44 74–5
   Polonaise Op.53 74
   Polonaise-Fantasie Op.61 75
   Prélude in B minor Op.28/6 136
   Prélude in E minor Op. 28/4 136
   Scherzo No.3 Op.39 9
   Sonata No.2 Op.35 63–4, 135
   [Funeral March]
Chopin, Justyna 2, 11
Chopin, Mikołaj 2, 11
Clésinger, Auguste 135, 137
Czartoryska, [Princess] Marcelina 129
Czartoryski, [Prince] Adam 4, 117, 136, 42n.16
Czartoryski, [Prince] Alexander 36
Czetwertyńska, [Princess] Louise 110–11
Czetwertyński, [Prince] Borys 110

Davison, James William 2, 148n.5
Delacroix, Eugène 34, 92, 48n.104, 136

Index

Dumas, Alexandre (*fils*) 30
 La Dame aux camélias 30–1
Duplessis, Marie 30, 47n.94

Eckhardt, Mária 13, 27
Elsner, Josef 116
Escudier M. [Publishers] 13

Fétis, François-Joseph 37
 Biographie universelle des musiciens 37
Fontana, Julian 117, 146n.23
Forkel, Johann Nikolaus 37–8
 On Johann Sebastian Bach's Life, Genius and Works 37
Fra Angelico 25
France musicale 13
Franchomme, August 136

Gathy, August 39, 49n.123
Gazette musicale 5
Glinka, Mikhail 18, 46n.69
 A Life for the Tsar 18
 Russlan and Ludmilla 18
Goethe, Johann Wolfgang von 23, 87, 95, 119, 123, 143n.5, 147n.7, 147n.20
Goldberg, Halina 8
Grzymała, Wojciech 12, 44n.48, 117
Gutmann, Adolphe 31, 129–30, 133, 135–6

Haynau, [General Baron] Ludwig 12, 44n.46
Heine, Heinrich 8, 26, 34, 90–1, 142n.8, 142n.12
 The Salon, or Letters on Art, Music, Popular Life and Politics 142n.7
Herder, Johann Gottfried 6, 14, 16, 19, 44n.54
Hiller, Ferdinand 91
 Destruction of Jerusalem 91
Hoffmann, E.T.A. 121

Horace 101
Hugo, Victor 34
Hummel, Johann Nepomuk 3, 116, 146n.21

Jean-Paul [Johann Paul Friedrich Richter] 65
Jędrzejewicz, Ludwika (*née* Chopin) 1, 11, 104, 132–4
Jelowicki, [Abbé] Alexandre 134–5

Kallberg, Jeffery 8
Korzuchowski, Antoine 108

Lablache, Luigi 136
La Fontaine, Jean de 62
Lamartine, Alphonse de 47n.93
Legouvé, Ernest 9
Lenz, Wilhelm von 41n.1
Licknowsky, [Prince] Félix 136, 150n.21
Lipinski, Karol Jozef 73, 140n.16
Liszt, Franz
 Fantasie romantique sur deux mélodies suisse 43n.30
 Funérailles 12, 26
 Historische ungarische Bildnisse 46n.80
 Hungarian Rhapsodies 7
 Magyar Dalok 7
 Magyar Rhapsódiák 7
 'On the Position of Artists and their Place in Society' 5, 42n.21
 Rondeau fantastique sur un thème espagnol 'El contrabandista' 43n.30
Lablache, Luigi 136
Lefébure-Wély, Louis 135–6
Louis-Philippe, [King] 4–5, 14, 42n.17
Luini, Bernardino 110, 146n.14

154

Index

Marcello, Benedetto 134
Mattheson, Johann 37, 48n.113
Mayseder, Joseph 73
Metternich, Clement von 14
Meyerbeer, Giacomo 91, 136
Mickiewicz, Adam 8, 15, 43n.31,
   62–3, 72, 92–3
  Dziady 62
  Grazyna 63
  Konrad Wallenrod 63
  Pan Tadeusz 72, 139n.12
Molin, [Dr.] Jean-Jacques 131
Mozart, Leopold 116
Mozart, Wolfgang Amadeus 1, 116, 135
  Don Giovanni 116
  Idomeneo 116
  Requiem 1, 135–6

Napoleon I [Emperor] 14–5
Napoleon III, [Emperor] 23
Nicholas I, [Tsar] 8, 45n.64
Niemcevicz, Julian 92
Nissen, [Baron] Georg von 37
Noailles, [Duc] Jules de 101
Nodier, Charles 85
  La Fée au miettes 85
  Les Lutins d'Argail 85
Nourrit, Adolphe 91

Ogiński's, [Prince] Michał 73, 139n.14
d'Ortigue, Joseph 13, 44n.51
Ossian 63, 71, 138n.8
Ostrowski, Jan 117, 146n.23
Ovid 78

Paganini, Nicolò 3, 36
Pękacz, Jolanta 8
Petrarch 61, 138n.5, 143n.20
Pindar 71
Pleyel, Camille 6, 89, 130, 137
Pleyel, Marie 42n.22

Potocka, [Countess] Delphine 117, 133–4, 146n.22
Pushkin, Alexander 143n.9
Radziwiłł, [Prince] Antoine 108
  Faust 108
Reber, Henri 135
Revue et gazette musicale 9
Rossini, Gioacchino 38–9
Rousseau, Jean-Jacques 19
Ruysdael, Jakob van 61

Sainte-Beuve, Charles 13, 33
Saint-Simon, [Comte] Claude Henri de 5
Sand, George 6, 11–12, 27–9,
   33–6, 43n.24, 92–3, 119–27
   passim, 128–9
  Horace 43n.26
  Lélia 119, 121, 146n.1
  Letters d'un voyageur 120–1
  Lucrezia Floriani 11, 27, 33–6,
   108–10, 115, 122, 124–5
  Spiridion 147n.16
  Un Hiver à Majorque 28–9
Sayn-Wittgenstein, [Princess]
  Caroyne von 2, 12, 24, 27,
  32–5, 41n.8
Sayn-Wittgenstein, [Princess] Marie von 27, 32
Schiller, Friedrich 132
  Die Ideale 132, 149n.10
Schindler, Anton 37–8
  Life of Beethoven 37–8
Schlesinger, Maurice 9
Schott [Publishers] 13
Schubert, Franz 61, 115
Schumann, Robert 8
Shakespeare, William 115
Słowacki, Juliusz 8, 43n.32
Sobieski, [King] Jan III 20, 66–7
Staël, [Baronne] Anne-Louise-Germaine de 128
Stradella, Alessandro 134

Index

Stendahl [Henri Behl] 37–9
   Vie de Rossini 37–9
Stirling, Jane 1, 11, 41n.4,
   41n.5
Suetonius 36
   On the Life of the Caesars 36

Tasso, Torquato 98, 143n.3
Trochimczyk, Maja 16

Vasari, Giorgio 37
   Lives of the Artists 37
Verdi 30
   La Traviata 30
Veronese, Paolo 67
Viardot, Pauline 136

Victoria, [Queen] 130
Voltaire 19

Wagner, Richard 22, 26, 46n.76
Walker, Alan 27
Weber, Carl Maria von 73–4
   Grande Polonaise Op.21
   140n.18
   Polacca Brillante (L'hilarité)
   Op.72 74, 140n.18
Weber, William 24
Wodsińska, Maria 28, 110

Zhukovsky, Vasily Andrevich
   143n.9
Żywny, Adalbert 107–8